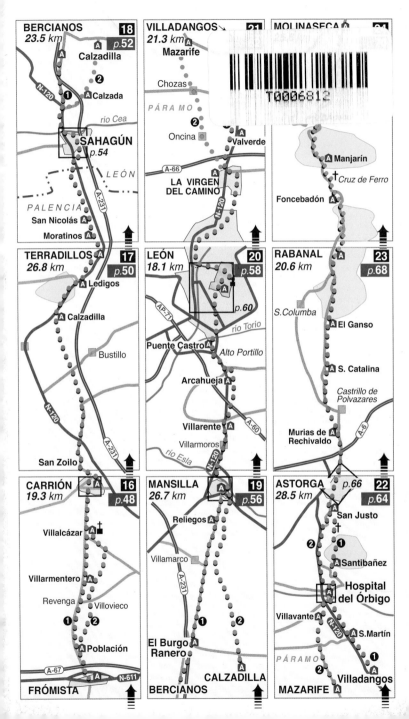

BERCIANOS 18
23.5 km p.52
Calzadilla
Calzada
río Cea
SAHAGÚN p.54
LEÓN
PALENCIA
San Nicolás
Moratinos
N-120
A-231

VILLADANGOS 21
21.3 km
Mazarife
Chozas
PÁRAMO
Oncina
Valverde
A-66
LA VIRGEN DEL CAMINO
N-120

MOLINASECA 24
Manjarín
Cruz de Ferro
Foncebadón

TERRADILLOS 17
26.8 km p.50
Ledigos
Calzadilla
Bustillo
N-120
San Zoilo
A-231

LEÓN 20
18.1 km p.58
p.60
río Torío
Puente Castro
Alto Portillo
Arcahueja
AP-71
Villarente
A-60
Villarmoros
río Esla
N-120

RABANAL 23
20.6 km p.68
S. Columba
El Ganso
S. Catalina
Castrillo de Polvazares
Murias de Rechivaldo
A-6

CARRIÓN 16
19.3 km p.48
Villalcázar
Villarmentero
Revenga
Villovieco
Población
A-67
N-611
FRÓMISTA

MANSILLA 19
26.7 km p.56
Reliegos
Villamarco
A-231
El Burgo Ranero
CALZADILLA
BERCIANOS

ASTORGA 22
28.5 km p.64
p.66
San Justo
Santibañez
Hospital del Órbigo
Villavante
S. Martín
N-120
PÁRAMO
Villadangos
MAZARIFE

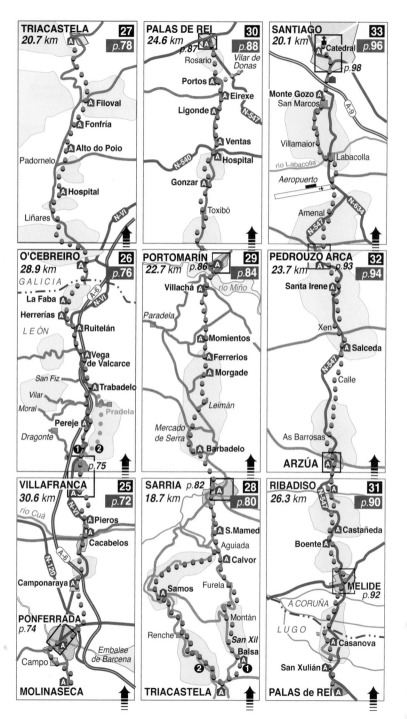

TRIACASTELA
20.7 km | **27** | *p.78*

Filoval
Fonfría
Alto do Poio
Padornelo
Hospital
Liñares

PALAS DE REI
24.6 km | **30** | *p.87* | *p.88*

Vilar de Donas
Rosario
Portos
Eirexe
Ligonde
Ventas
Hospital
Gonzar
Toxibó

SANTIAGO
20.1 km | **33** | Catedral | *p.96* | *p.98*

Monte Gozo
San Marcos
Villamaior
Labacolla
río Labacolla
Aeropuerto
Amenal
N-634
N-547

O'CEBREIRO
28.9 km | **26** | *p.76*

GALICIA
La Faba
Herrerías
LEÓN
Ruitelán
Vega de Valcarce
San Fiz
Vilar
Moral
Trabadelo
Pereje
Dragonte
Pradela
1 **2**
p.75

PORTOMARÍN
22.7 km | **29** | *p.86* | *p.84*

río Miño
Villachá
Paradela
Momientos
Ferrerios
Morgade
Leimán
Mercado de Serra
Barbadelo

PEDROUZO ARCA
23.7 km | **32** | *p.93* | *p.94*

Santa Irene
Xen
Salceda
Calle
As Barrosas
ARZÚA

VILLAFRANCA
30.6 km | **25** | *p.72*

río Cúa
Pieros
Cacabelos
Camponaraya
PONFERRADA
p.74
Campo
Embalse de Barcena
MOLINASECA

SARRIA *p.82*
18.7 km | **28** | *p.80*

S.Mamed
Aguiada
Calvor
Furela
Samos
Montán
Renche
San Xil
Balsa
2 **1**
TRIACASTELA

RIBADISO
26.3 km | **31** | *p.90*

Castañeda
Boente
MELIDE
p.92
A CORUÑA
LUGO
Casanova
San Xulián
PALAS de REI

Camino de Santiago

Camino Francés
St. Jean Pied de Port – Santiago

maps - mapas - mappe
mapy - karten - cartes

John Brierley

© John Brierley 2008, 2009, 2013, 2014, 2015, 2016, 2017, 2018, 2019, 2020, 2022, 2022/3 © John Brierley & Gemma Brierley 2024

ISBN: 978-1-912216-34-5

British Library Cataloguing-in-Publication Data.
A catalogue record for this book is available from the British Library.

All photographs © John Brierley & Gemma Brierley 2024
All maps © John Brierley & Gemma Brierley 2024

Printed and bound in Czechia

Published by
CAMINO GUIDES
An imprint of Kaminn Media Ltd
272 Bath Street,
Glasgow, G2 4JR

Tel: +44 (0)141 354 1758
Fax: +44 (0)141 354 1759

Email: info@caminoguides.com
www.caminoguides.com

About the Author: John Brierley 1948 - 2023

After more than a quarter of a century walking and working on the caminos John took the final steps on his earthly pilgrimage in 2023. For more than a decade he shared the work of Camino Guides with his daughter, Gemma, who continues to keep them updated in his memory.

St Jean Pied de Port – Santiago de Compostela 778.5 km (483.7 miles)

33 Stages / Etapas / Stufen / Stadi / Estágios / Étapes / Etapy

MAP LEGEND: Symbols & Abbreviations

Total km *equiv.*	Total distance for stage
	Adjusted for cumulative climb (each 100m vertical +10 mins)
(850m) **Alto** ▲	Contours / High point of each stage
< 🅐 🅗 >	Intermediate accommodation ❷ (*often less busy / quieter*)
3.5 ➤	Precise distance between points (3.5 km = ± 1 hour)
◦ 50m > / ^ / <	Interim distances 50m right> / s/o=straight on^ / <left
,,,,,,,,,,,,,,,	Natural path / forest track / gravel *senda*
	Quiet country lane (asphalt)
══○══	Secondary road (*grey*: asphalt) / Roundabout *rotonda*
══N-11══	Main road [N-] *Nacional* (*red*: additional traffic and hazard)
══A-1══	Motorway *autopista* (*blue*: conventional motorway colour)
++++++●	Railway *ferrocarril* / Station *estación*
●●●●●●	Main Waymarked route (*yellow*: ± 80% of pilgrims)
●●●●●●	Alternative Scenic route (*green*: more remote / less pilgrims)
●●●●●●	Alternative road route (*grey*: more asphalt & traffic)
◦◦◦◦◦◦	Optional detour *desvío* (*turquoise*: to point of interest)
▓▒░▒░▒	Primary Path of pilgrimage (**purple**: inner path of Soul)
☒ ❓ ❗	Crossing *cruce* / Option *opción* / Extra care ¡cuidado!
🌾 ☀ 📡	Windmill *molino* / Viewpoint *punto de vista* / Radio mast
▪━▪/▪━▪	National boundary / Provincial boundary *límite provincial*
∼/∼	River *río* / Riverlet Stream *arroyo* / *rego*
◯	Sea or lake *Mar o lago* / Woodland *bosques*
⛪ ⚰ ✝	Church *iglesia* / Chapel *capilla* / Wayside cross *cruceiro*
🅕 ☕ 🛒	Drinking font *fuente* / Café / Shop (*mini*)*mercado*
🍴 *menú* V.	Restaurant / *menú peregrino* / *V. Vegetariano(a)*
ℹ 🏛 ✕	Tourist office *turismo* / Manor house *pazo* / Rest area *picnic*
➕ ✚ ✉	Pharmacy *farmacia* / Hospital / Post office *correos*
✈ 🚌 ⛽	Airport / Bus station *estación de autobús* / *gasolinera*
⁙ *XIIc.*	Ancient monument / 12th century
🅷 🅿 🅒	Hotels •*H-H*** €30-90 / Pension •*P** €20-35 / •*CR (B&B)* €35-75
x12 €35-45	Number of private rooms *x12* €35(single)-45 (double) *approx*
🄷 🄰 🄰	*Off* route lodging / 🄰 Reported closed - check for updates
🄰❶❷ 🄹	Pilgrim hostel(s) *Albergue* ●*Alb.* + Youth hostel ●*Juventude*
[32]	Number of bed spaces (usually bunk beds *literas*) €5-€17
[÷4] +12	÷ number of dormitories / *+12* number of private rooms €30+
Par.	Parish hostel *Parroquial* donation *donativo* / €5
Conv.	Convent or monastery hostel *donativo* / €5
Mun/Xunta	Municipal hostel €5+ / Galician government *Xunta* €8
Asoc.	Association hostel €8+
Priv. (*)	Private hostel (network*) €10-17
	[all prices average (low season) for comparison purposes only]
p.55	Town plan *plan de la ciudad* with page number
(Pop.– Alt. m)	Town population – altitude in metres
▭	City suburbs / outskirts *afueras* (*grey*)
	Historical centre *centro histórico / barrio antiguo* (*brown*)

Introduction: We have too much paraphernalia in our lives. This slim maps only edition seeks to lighten the load. This has been made possible by the selfless work of pilgrim associations that have waymarked all routes. It is difficult to get lost if we remain present to each moment and attentive for the yellow arrows that point the way to Santiago – mindfulness is the key. However, this *maps only* version cannot substitute for the more detailed information contained in the full guide, which features details of •*alternative routes* •*lodging* •*historical notes* and •*intimations of the mystical path.* The full guide is now available in both print and eBook format, meaning a digital version can be downloaded and referred to prior to setting out on the path each day while these handy maps can be kept in your pocket.

Before using this guide take time to familiarise yourself with the map symbols & abbreviations opposite. For notes on preparation for both the inner journey and practical notes on packing and travel see the full guide *A Pilgrim's Guide to the Camino Francés* or the Preparation page on our website *www.caminoguides.com*

All of us travel two paths simultaneously; the outer path along which we haul our body and the inner pathway of soul. We need to be mindful of both and take time to prepare ourselves accordingly. The traditional way of the pilgrim is to travel alone, by foot, carrying all the material possessions we might need for the journey ahead. This provides the first lesson for the pilgrim – to leave behind all that is superfluous and to travel with only the barest necessities. Preparation for the inner path is similar – we start by letting go of psychic waste accumulated over the years; resentments, prejudices and outmoded belief systems. With an open mind and open heart we will more readily assimilate the lessons to be found along this ancient Path of Enquiry.

We have been asleep a long time. Despite the chaotic world around us, or perhaps because of it, something is stirring us to awaken from our collective amnesia. A sign of this awakening is the number of people drawn to walk the caminos. The hectic pace of modern life, experienced not only in our work but also our family and social lives, spins us ever outwards away from our centre. We have allowed ourselves to be thrown onto the surface of our lives – mistaking busy-ness for aliveness, but this superficial existence is inherently purposeless.

Pilgrimage offers us an opportunity to slow down and allow some spaciousness into our lives. In this quieter space we can reflect on the deeper significance of our lives and the reasons why we came here. The camino encourages us to ask the perennial question – who am I? And, crucially, it provides time for answers to be understood and integrated. Don't rush the camino – take the time it takes because it may well prove a pivotal turning point in your life. Whichever route we take, our ultimate Destination is assured. The only real choice we have is how long it takes us to arrive...

buen camino – John Brierley

ST. JEAN PIED de PORT *(pop. 1,800 – alt. 170m)* ❶ *Office de Tourisme* ©0559 370 357 / © **France +33.** ● Pilgrim Passport: *Carnet de Pelerin / Credencial* ✣ *Accueil pèlerins* © 0559 370 509 *rue de la Citadelle (N°39)* (07:30–12:30 / 13:30–22:00). **Pilgrim Equipment:** ✣ *Boutique du pélerin (N°32)* © 0559 379 852 / 06:30–19:00. **Backpack transfer & transport:** ✣ *Express Bourricot (N°31)* © 0661 960 476 *www.expressbourricot.com* & Jean Paul © 0622577486 *www.napoleon-compostelle.fr*

○ **Monuments historiques:** *medieval rue de la Citadelle.* ❶ *Porte St Jacques XV* (UNESCO). ❷ *Citadelle (Table d'Orientation).* ❸ *La Maison des Evêques XVI.* ❹ *Porte de France* rue Eglise. ❺ *Porte de Navarre.* ❻ *Notre Dame du Bout du Pont XIV.* ❼ *Porte D'Espagne.*

Porte Saint-Jacques
Albergue ❶ Municipal

● *Albergues* ◖Rue de la Citadelle *N°55»* ❶ Municipal *[32÷3]* €12 incl. *N°51»* ❷ Porte Saint-Jacques *[6÷2]* €20 ©630 997 561. *N°50»* ❸ Azkorria *Priv.[8÷2]+* €28+ © 676 020 536. *N°40»* ❹ Bellari *Priv.[14÷4]* €40 ½-board © 0559 372 468. *N°36»* ❺ Au Chant du Coq *Priv.[8]+* €15 © 0674 310 283. *N°35»* ❻ Makila *Priv. [8÷2]* €25 +2 €65 © 0663 101 346. *N°29»* ❼ Esteban Etxea *[12÷1]* €19 +2 © 663 629 235. *N°30»* ❽ Le Lièvre et La Tortue *[15÷2]* €20 +1 © 663 629 235. *N°8»* ❾ Gite Ultreïa *Priv.*[11÷2]* €23 +2 €56 © 0680 884 622. ◖Rue d'Espagne *N°11»* ❿ Bidean *Priv.[12]* €18 © 670 296 666. *N°21»* ⓫ Le Chemin Vers L'Etoile *Priv.[46÷5]* €18+ © 0559 372 071. *N°43»* ⓬ Maison Kaserna *Par.[14÷2]* €22 incl. © 0559 376 517 ⓭ Zuharpeta *Priv.[15÷1]* €28 incl. +4 €75 © 0559 373 588 rue Zuharpeta 5. ◖Otros: ⓮ Compostella *Priv.[14÷5]* €20 © 0559 370 236 rue d'Arneguy. ⓯ La Vita é Bella *[10÷2]* €17 © 768 234 007. ⓰ Gite Izaxulo *[18÷3]* €20 +2 €72 © 524 341 900 2 Av. Renaud, 2.

● *Hotels:* ◖Rue de la Citadelle •*H* Plan B *x5* €50+ •*H* Maison E.Bernat *x3* €110+ © 621 328 641. •*H* Maison Simonenia *x8* 559 375 610. ◖Rua France •*H¨*Ramuntcho *x16* €80+ © 0559 370 391. ◖Place Charles de Gaulle •*H¨*Central *x14* €95 © 0559 370 022. •*H¨¨*Les Pyrénées *x18* €100+ © 0559 370 101 ◖Place du Trinquet •*H¨*Itzalpea *x7* €80 © 0559 370 366. •*H¨* La Villa Esponda *x4* €60 © 621 141 079. •*H¨*Les Remparts *x9* €70 © 0559 371 379, Place Floquet •Maison Ziberoa €60+ © 661 235 944 route d'arnéguy.

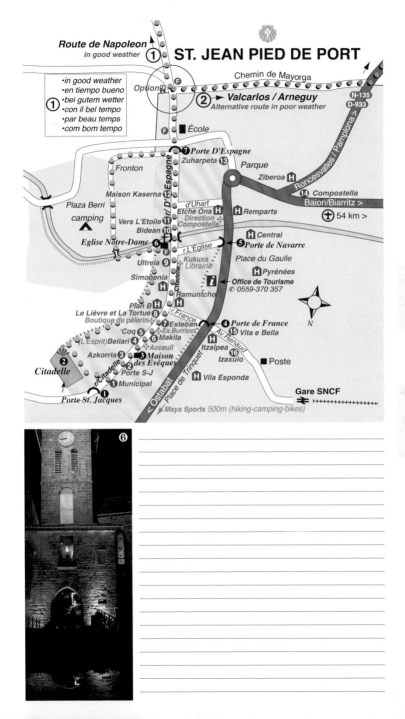

ST. JEAN PIED DE PORT

Route de Napoleon *in good weather* ①

Chemin de Mayorga

Option ① ②

► **Valcarlos / Arneguy**
Alternative route in poor weather

N-135
D-933

- in good weather
- en tiempo bueno
- bei gutem wetter ①
- con il bel tempo
- par beau temps
- com bom tempo

École

❼ **Porte D'Espagne**

Zuharpeta ⑬

Parque

Fronton

Ziberoa ⌂

Maison Kaserna ⑫

⑭ **Compostella**

Baion/Biarritz ›

Plaza Berri
camping ▲

d'Uhart

Etche Ona ⌂ ⌂ **Remparts**

Vers L'Etoile ⑪ Direction Compostelle

✚ 54 km ›

Bidean ⑩

Eglise Notre-Dame ❻

r.L'Eglise

⌂ **Central**

❺ **Porte de Navarre**

Ultreia ⑨

Kukuxa Librairie

Place du Gaulle

Simoñenia ⌂

⌂ **Pyrénées**

Ramuntcho

ℹ **Office de Tourisme**
© 0559-370 357

Plan B ⌂

Le Lièvre et La Tortue ❽
Boutique du pèlerin ✚

r.France

N

❹ **Porte de France**

'Coq ⑤ ✚Ex.Burricot Esteban ❼

⑮ **Vita e Bella**

(L'Esprit)Beilari ④ ❻ **Makila**

Av.Renaud

Itzalpea

Acceuil

Izaxulo ⑯

■ **Poste**

Azkorria ③ ■❸ **Maison des Evêques**

❷ Porte S-J

Citadelle ❷

r.Citadelle

❶ **Municipal**

⌂ ❾ **Vila Esponda**

Gare SNCF
⇄

Porte St. Jacques ❶

Maya Sports 500m (hiking-camping-bikes)

❻

01 ST. JEAN PIED-de-PORT – RONCESVALLES

ⓒ France + 33   ⓒ España + 34
ⓒ Emergency Europe 112

....	--- --- 12.4 --- ---	49%
	--- --- 12.7 --- ---	51%
▬▬▬	--- --- 0.0	
Total km	--- --- **25.1** km	*(15.6 ml)*

Total ascent **1,390**m ± *2¼ hr*
Alto ▲ Col de Loepeder **1,450**m *(4,757 ft)*
< Ⓐ Ⓗ > ➲Huntto **5.4** km ➲Orisson **7.8** km

Vierge
d'Orisson

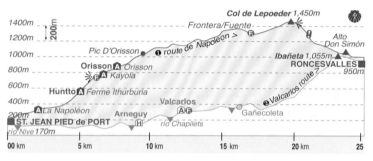

❶ *Route de Napoleon* ● St. Jean Pied-de-Port: ●*Auberge* La Coquille Napoleón *Priv.[10÷1]* €18 +2 €55 (menú€12) ⓒ 0662 259 940. •Villa Goxoki ⓒ 0559 491 773. ● Gite Antton *[14÷3]* €22 ⓒ 982 551 320. ▌Huntto •*Auberge* Ferme Ithurburia *Priv.[17÷4]*€20 +5 €70 ⓒ 0559 37. ▌Orisson •*Gite* Kayola *Priv. [15÷1]* €17 + ●*Auberge* Orrison *Priv.* *[28÷4]* €42 *(½ board)* ⓒ 0559 491 303 *www.refuge-orisson.com* ●Borda *Priv.* *[12÷3]*+ €42 *(½ board)* ⓒ 661 929 743.

❷ *Route de Valcarlos:* ▌Arneguy •*H¨* Clementia *x9* €46-€60 ⓒ 0559 371 354. ▌Valcarlos *Luzaide* ●*Alb.* Municipal *[24÷2]* ⓒ 646 048 883. •*CR* Etxezuria *x8* €50 ⓒ 948 790 01 *www.etxezuria.com* •*CR* Erlanio *x3* €55 ⓒ 948 790 218 •*Hs* Maitena *x6* €45-€55 ⓒ 948 790 210.

● Roncesvalles ●*Alb.* Roncesvalles *Conv.[183÷4]* ⓒ 948 760 + *credencial del peregrino 10:00 - 22.00* •*H¨¨* Roncesvalles *x16* €59-€92 & *Apartamentos* •los Beneficiados ⓒ 948 760 105 *www.hotelroncesvalles.com* •*Hs* Casa Sabina *x4* €45 ⓒ 948 760 012. •*Hs* La Posada *x20* €68+ ⓒ 948 790 322.

Albergue
Roncesvalles

02 RONCESVALLES – ZUBIRI

....	--- --- 17.5 --- ---	80%
▬▬▬	--- --- 3.2 --- ---	15%
▬▬	--- --- 1.2 --- ---	5%
Total km	**21.9** km (*13.6 ml*)	

Total ascent **250**m ± ½ **hr**
Alto ▲ Alto de Mezquíriz **955**m (*3,133* ft)
< 🅐 🅗 > ➲Burguete *Auritz* **3.1** km ➲Espinal
Aurizberri **6.7**km ➲Viskarreta **11.8** km

■ **Burguete** *Auritz:* ●*Alb* **Lorentx Aterpea** *Priv.[42÷7]* €15 © 948 032 127.
•*Hs¨* **Burguete** *x12* €40+ © 948 790 005 •*CR* **Txikipolit** *x3* €60 ©948 760 019.
•*CR* **Iturrialdea** *x4* €28 ©948 760 243. •*CR* **Jauregui** *x7* €55 ©948 760 031.
•*CR* **Bergara** *x5* €50 © 948 760 044. •*CR* **Pedroarena** *x6* €40 ©619 444 207.
•*H¨¨* **Loizu** *x27* €55-€90 ©948 760 008. [● +1.6km ▲*Alb* **Urrobi** *[42÷6]* €13]
■**Espinal** *Aurizberri:* ●*Alb* **Haizea** *Priv.[26÷2]* €12 +*12* €65 © 948 760 379
www.hostalhaizea.com ●*Alb.* **Irugoienea** *Priv.[21÷2]* €12 +*3* €45 © 649 412 487
www.irugoienea.com •*CR* **Patxikuzuria** *x3* €20–€60 © 948 760 167 ■ **Viscarreta**
Bizkarreta: •*CR* **La Posada Nueva** *x8* €40 ©699 131 433. •*CR* **Batit** €20 © 616
068 347 c/ S.Pedro. •*CR* **Maitetxu** *x5* €45-65 ©948 760 175. ■ **Linzoain** •*CR*
Posada El Camino *x4* €40+ © 622 688 535
● **ZUBIRI:** *Alb.* ❶ **río Arga Ibaia** *Priv.[8÷2]* €15 +*2* €40 © 948 304 243. ❷
Zaldiko *Priv.[24÷3]* €14 © 609 736 420. ❸ **El Palo de Avellano** *Priv.[59÷5]* €18
+*3* €62 © 666 499 175 www.elpalodeavellano.com. ❹ **Segunda Etapa** *Priv.[12÷2]*
€15 © 697 186 560. ❺ **Antigua Escuela** *Muni.[46÷6]* €8 © 628 324 186 Av. Zubiri
[+300m]. ❻ **Suseia** *Priv.[20÷4]* €15 +*3* © 948 304 353 www.alberguesuseia.com
C/ Murelu, 12 *[+500m].* •*P¨* **Zubiaren Etxea** *x4* © 948 304 293.•*P¨* **Usoa** *x5* €25-
€38 © 628 058 048.•*P¨* **Amets** *x4* €45-€55 © 618 636 189 with garden by river. On
main road •*P¨* **Goika** © 638 847 974. •*P¨* **Benta Berri** *x4* © 636 134 781 & •*Hs¨*
Zubiri © 948 304 329 *from* €60-€100. •*Hs* **Gau-Txori** *x7* €42-59 © 948 30 45 31
www.hostalgautxori.com •*CR* **Txantxorena** *x8* €68 © 679 129 396.

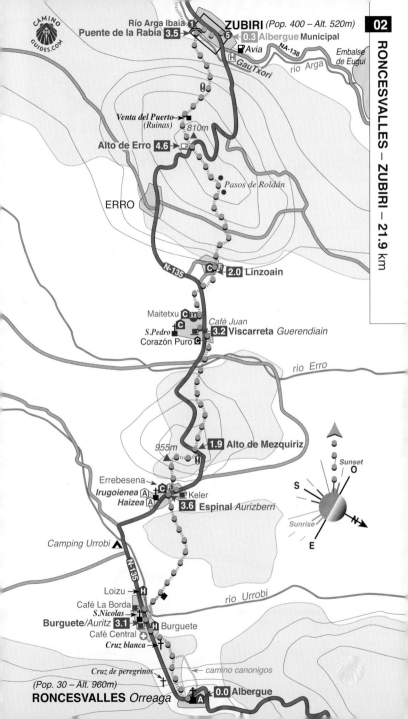

Río Arga Ibaia **1**
Puente de la Rabia 3.5 →
ZUBIRI *(Pop. 400 – Alt. 520m)*
5 **0.3** Albergue Municipal
Avia
Gau Txori

Embalse de Eugui

rio Arga
NA-138

Venta del Puerto →
(Ruinas)
810m

Alto de Erro 4.6 →

ERRO

Pasos de Roldán

N-135

C F **2.0** **Linzoain**

Maitetxu **C m**
C
S.Pedro →
Corazón Puro **C**

Café Juan
3.2 **Viscarreta** *Guerendiain*

río Erro

955m

1.9 **Alto de Mezquiriz**

Errebesena →
Irugoienea **A** **C F**
Haizea **A**
Keler
3.6 **Espinal** *Aurizberri*

Camping Urrobi ▲

N-135

río Urrobi

Loizu **H**
Café La Borda
S.Nicolas →
Burguete/Auritz 3.1
Café Central →
Cruz blanca →

H Burguete

Cruz de peregrinos
camino canonigos

(Pop. 30 – Alt. 960m)
RONCESVALLES *Orreaga*

A **0.0** Albergue

Sunset O

S

N

Sunrise

E

CAMINO GUIDES.COM

03 ZUBIRI – PAMPLONA

▦	--- --- 13.3 --- --- *64%*
▬	--- --- 2.2 --- --- *11%*
▬	--- --- 5.4 --- --- *25%*
Total km	**20.9** km (*13.0 ml*)

Total ascent **360**m ± ½ *hr*
Alto ▲ Ilarratz **560**m (*1,837 ft*)
< 🅰 🏠 > ➲Larrasoaña **5.3**km ➲Zuriain **9.1**km
➲*Zabaldika 12.7km (+0.3)* ➲Trinidad de Arre / Villalba **16.1**km ➲*Huarte 16.6km*

■ **Illaratz** ●*Alb.* **Ezpeleku** *Priv.[6÷1]*+ €15+48 c/ San Martín, 3 ©696 808 894
■ **Urdániz** (*+ 0.5 km*) •*Hs* **Acá y Allá** *Priv.[10÷2]* €20 + piscina ©615 257 666
(Jesús Góngora) c/ San Miguel 18.

● **Larrasoaña:** 🍴 *Taberna Perutxena. Alb.* ❶ **Larrasoaña** *Muni.[10÷2]* €8 ©
626 718 417 •*CR* **Tau** *x4* €50+ © 622 745 620 c/ Errotabidea 18. *Alb.* ❷ **San
Nicolás** *Priv.[40÷8]* €14 © 619 559 225 *www.alberguesannicolas.com* (Luis y
María Jesús) adj. 🍴 *mercado Amari* also ❸ **Asteia** *Priv.[12÷2]*+ €15 © 948 060
411 *www.asteiahostel.com* - **cerrado**. •*P'* **El Peregrino** *x4* €70 © 948 304 554) and
•*CR* **Casa Elita** *x3* €60 © 629 412 120 c/ Amairu 7.

■ **Akerreta:** •*H'''* **Akerreta** *x11* €60-90 ©948 304 572 *www.hotelakerreta.com*
■ **Zuriáin:** 🍴/●*Alb.* **La Parada de Zuriain** *Priv.[7÷2]* €13 incl.+3 €50 © 699
556 741. ● **Zabaldika:** ●*Alb.* **Zabaldika** *Par.[18÷3]* €-donativo ©948 330 918.
■ **Arre** *Puente río Ultzama:* ●*Alb.* **Cofradía de la Trinidad de Arre** *Conv.[34÷4]*
€10 *Hermanos Maristas* ©948 332 941. ■ **Villava** ●*Alb.* **Villava** *Muni.[54÷5]*
€14 ©948 517 731 c/Pedro de Atarrabia [+200m]. •*H'''* **Villava Pamplona** *x62*
€50+ ©948 333 676. •*P'* **Obel** *x6* €28-55+ ©948 126 056. 🍴 *Paradiso.* ■ **Burlada**
•*H''* **Burlada** *x53* €45 ©948 131 300.

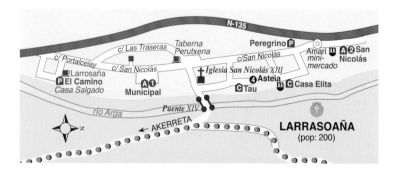

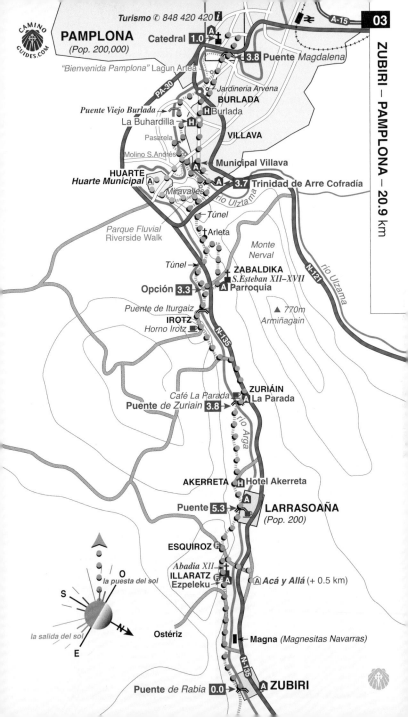

CAMINO GUIDES.COM

PAMPLONA
(Pop. 200,000)

Turismo © 848 420 420 **ℹ**

A-15

Catedral **1.0** **A** ✝ Catedral

3.8 Puente *Magdalena*

"Bienvenida Pamplona" Lagun Artea

PA-30

Jardineria Arvena

BURLADA

Puente Viejo Burlada → **H** Burlada

La Buhardilla **H**

VILLAVA

Pasarela

Molino S.Andrés

A Municipal Villava

HUARTE
Huarte Municipal **A**

A 3.7 **Trinidad de Arre Cofradía**

Miravalles

río Ulzama

Parque Fluvial
Riverside Walk

Túnel

✝ *Arleta*

Monte Nerval

río Ulzama

N-121

Túnel

ZABALDIKA
■ *S.Esteban XII–XVII*

Opción 3.3 **A** Parroquia

▲ *770m Armiñagain*

Puente de Iturgaiz

IROTZ
Horno Irotz ■

N-135

ZURIÁIN

Café La Parada → **A** La Parada

Puente de Zuriain 3.8 →

río Arga

AKERRETA **H** Hotel Akerreta

A

Puente 5.3 → **A** **LARRASOAÑA**
(Pop. 200)

ESQUIROZ ┌F┐

Abadia XII ✝
ILLARATZ ┌F┐ **A**
Ezpeleku **A** *Acá y Allá* (+ 0.5 km)

O
la puesta del sol
S

NO

E
la salida del sol

Ostériz

■ → **Magna** *(Magnesitas Navarras)*

N-135

Puente de Rabia 0.0 → **A ZUBIRI**

PAMPLONA pop. 200,000 (Codex Calixtinus III).
❶ *Turismo*, Av. Roncesvalles, 4 ℂ 848 420 420 (10.00-17.00 / 10.00-14.00).
❖ *Caminoteca* c/Curia, 15 ℂ Itsván & Anita 948 210 316.

❶ **Puente de Magdalena** *XII.* ❷ **Portal de Francia** *(Zumalacárregi)* ● **Baluarte del Redín** *rincón y cruz de Menidero.* ❸ **Catedral de Santa María la Real** *XV Claustro / Puerta Preciosa / Diocesan museu (€2 + credencial).* ● **Plaza de Toros** Paseo Ernest Hemingway. ● **S. Bartolomé Fortín** *XVII.* ● **Plaza del Castillo.** ❹ **Iglesia San Nicolás** *XII* c/San Nicolás & c/San Miguel. ❺ **San Saturnino** *(San Cernín) XIII* ❻ **Casa Consistorial** *(encierros).* ❼ *Museo de Navarra* c/Santo Domingo. ❽ **Iglesia San Lorenzo** *(y Capela de San Fermín).* ❾ **Ciudadela.**

● *Albergues Centro:* ❶ Casa Paderborn *Asoc.[26÷5]* €7 ℂ *948 211 712 jakobusfreunde-paderborn.com Playa de Caparroso, 6.* ❷ Ibarrola *Priv.[20÷1]* €18 incl. ℂ *948 223 332 www.casaibarrola.com* c/ Carmen, Nº31 @Nº18 ❸ Iruñako Aterpea *Priv.[22÷2]* €15 +*1* €40 ℂ 948 044 637 ❹ Jesús y María *Asoc.[112÷2]* €11 ℂ 948 222 644 *Iglesia Jesús y María XVII* c/ Compañía. ❺ Plaza Catedral *Priv.[38÷3]* €18 +*2* €50 ℂ 948 591 336 *www.albergueplazacatedral.com* c/ Navarrería 35. ❻ Betania *[14÷2]* € *donativo,* Calle Recoletas, 1-2

● *Hostels:* (€15+): ● Aloha *[26÷4]* €15 c/Sangüesa,2 ℂ 948 153 367. ● Juvenil *youth hostel* c/Goroabe, 36.

● *Hoteles Centro:* •*H¨¨¨¨* Pamplona Catedral €70+ ℂ 948 226 688 c/ Dos de Mayo. •*P˙* Lambertini ℂ 948 210 303. •*H¨¨¨¨* La Perla €140+ ℂ 948 223 000 Plaza del Castillo). •*Hs¨* Arriazu *x20* €60 ℂ 948 210 202 c. de las Comedias, 14. ❮San Nicolás*: Nº2»* •*P˙* Otano ℂ 948 227 036. *Nº24»* •*Hs* Don Lluis ℂ 948 210 499. ❮San Gregorio*: Nº1²* •*P˙* El Camino *x10* €40+ ℂ 638 206 664. *Nº2»* •*P˙* La Montañesa ℂ 948 224 380. •*P¨* El Paseo *x8* €45+ ℂ 948 223 084 c/ Sarasate, 30. •*P* Escaray *x7* €45 c/Nueva, 24 ℂ 948 227 825. •*H¨* Eslava *x28* single room from €38 double room €60+ ℂ 948 221 558 Plaza Virgen de la O. •*H¨¨¨¨* Tres Reyes €89+ ℂ 948 22 66 00 Jardines de la Taconera.

● *Otros Hoteles:* •*P˙* Leyre *x6* €45+ ℂ 948 211 647 *www.pensionleyre.com.* ❮Avenida Pio XII: *Nº43»* •*H¨¨¨¨* Blanca Navarra €75+ ℂ 948 17 10 10. *Nº32»* •*P˙* Pasadena *x10* €39+ ℂ 948 177 650. •*H* Hostal Acella *x31* €40 ℂ 948 261 000 *www.hostalacella.com* ajd.•*P* Pamplonabeds *x9* €42 ℂ 948 256 366 Trav. Acella 2/3.

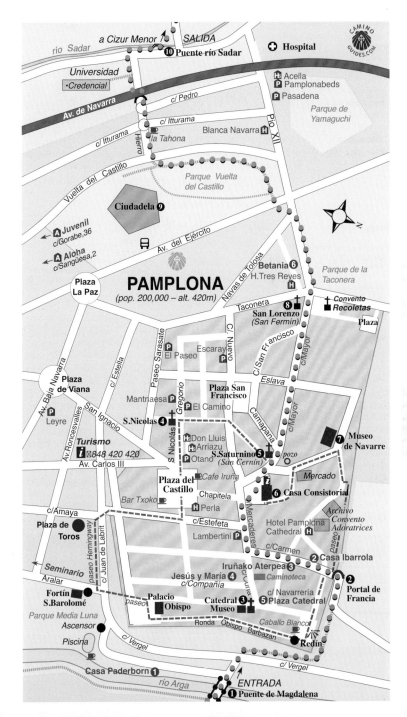

04 PAMPLONA – PUENTE LA REINA

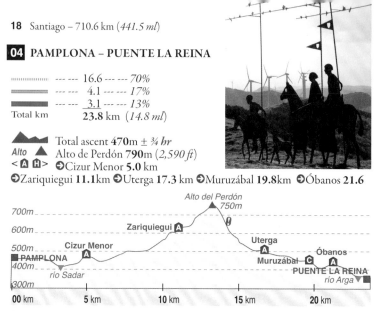

⋯⋯⋯⋯	--- --- 16.6 --- ---	70%
━━━	--- --- 4.1 --- ---	17%
▬▬▬	--- --- 3.1 --- ---	13%
Total km	23.8 km (*14.8 ml*)	

▲ Total ascent **470**m ± ¾ *hr*

Alto ▲ Alto de Perdón **790**m (*2,590 ft*)

< 🅰 🅗 > ↪Cizur Menor **5.0** km

↪Zariquiegui **11.1**km ↪Uterga **17.3** km ↪Muruzábal **19.8**km ↪Óbanos **21.6**

Elevation profile:
- 700m
- Alto del Perdón 750m
- 600m — Zariquiegui 🅰
- θ
- 500m — Cizur Menor 🅰 — Uterga 🅰
- PAMPLONA ▪ — Muruzábal 🅲 — Óbanos 🅰
- 400m — río Sadar — PUENTE LA REINA río Arga ▼▪
- 300m
- 00 km   5 km   10 km   15 km   20 km

▪ **Cizur Menor:** Iglesia de San Miguel Arcángel *XII*. *Alb.*❶ **Orden de Malta** *Priv.* *[27÷1]* €7 ✆ 616 651 330 Orden de San Juan de Malta. *Alb.*❷ **Roncal** *Priv.* *[50÷5]* €13 Maribel Roncal ✆ 670 323 271. ● *Cizur Mayor* Zizur Maior: (+1.5 km). •*H*ˈˈ **Casa Azcona** *x21* €58+ ✆ 948 287 662 •*Hs* **Ardoi** *x9* €35-50 ✆ 948 185 044 •*H*ˈˈˈˈ**Zizur** *x78* €68+ ✆ 948 287 119 ▮ **Zariquiegui:** ●*Alb* **San Andrés** *Priv.[18÷2]* €10 ✆ 948 353 876 + 🍴. ▮ **Uterga:** c/Mayor ●*Alb.* **Camino del Perdón** *Priv.[16÷1]* €12 +3 €60 ✆ 948 344 598 www.caminodelperdon.es 🛒 menú. ●*Alb.* **Casa Baztan** *Priv.[24÷1]* €10 +2 €45 ✆ 948 344 528. •*Hs* **Camino del Perdón** *x5* €60 ✆ 948 344 598. ▮ **Muruzábal:** *Alb.*❶ **El Jardín de Muruzábal** *Priv.[14÷1]* €10 +4 €50 ✆ 696 688 399 www.eljardindemuruzabal.com *Alb.*❷ **Mendizabal** *Priv.[12÷4]* €12 +€30 ✆ 948 344 631. *CR* **Villazón I** €45 ✆948 277 391 www.casavillazon.com. 🍴🛒 Nogales. ●*Eunate:* (+2.4 km) Iglesia Santa María de Eunate *XII.* ▮ **Óbanos:** ●*Alb.* **Usda** *Priv.[42÷3]* €9 ✆ 676 560 927 ●*Alb.* **Atseden** *Priv.[12÷1]* €13 incl. ✆ 646 924 912 www.atsedenhostel.com •*Hs* **Mamerto** *x9* €30-45 ✆ 948 344 344 c/San Lorenze 13. •*CR* **Villazón II** €35-45 ✆948 277 391 •*CR* **Raichu** *x5* €27-45 ✆ 948 344 285 www.casaraichu.com
● **Puente La Reina** *p.20*

Santa María de Eunate

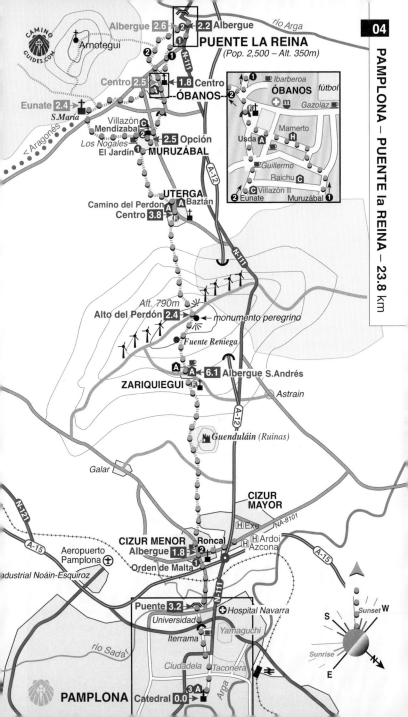

Albergue 2.6 — 2 — 2.2 Albergue

PUENTE LA REINA
(Pop. 2,500 – Alt. 350m)

río Arga

Arnotegui

Centro 2.5 — 1.8 Centro
ÓBANOS

Eunate 2.4
S.María

Villazón
Mendizabal C
Los Nogales
El Jardín 2.5 Opción
MURUZÁBAL

< Aragonés

ÓBANOS fútbol

Ibarberoa
Gazolaz
Usda A Mamerto H
Guillermo
Raichu C
Villazón II
Eunate Muruzábal

UTERGA Baztán
Camino del Perdon
Centro 3.8

N-111

A-12

Alt. 790m
Alto del Perdón 2.4 → ● *monumento peregrino*

● *Fuente Reniega*

A — A 6.1 Albergue S.Andrés
ZARIQUIEGUI
Astrain

Guenduláin (Ruinas)

Galar

CIZUR MAYOR

Exe NA-8101

Ardoi
Azcona

CIZUR MENOR Roncal
Albergue 1.8
Aeropuerto
Pamplona ✈
Orden de Malta

Industrial Noáin-Esquíroz

N-121
A-15

Puente 3.2 → Hospital Navarra
Universidad
Iterrama Yamaguchi

río Sada
Ciudadela Taconera
Arga

PAMPLONA Catedral 0.0 → 3 A

Sunset W
S
Sunrise
E

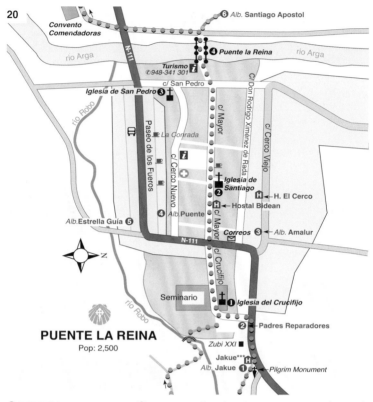

PUENTE LA REINA
Pop: 2,500

● **PUENTE LA REINA:** ❶ *Turismo* ℂ 948 341 301 c/ Mayor (Puente).
◖**Albergues:** ❶ **Jakue** *Priv.*[40÷2]* €14 + *H**** Jakue €45 ℂ 948 341 017 *www.jakue.com Alb.* ❷ **Padres Reparadores** *Conv.[100÷12]* €7 ℂ 948 340 050 c/ Crucifijo. *Alb.* ❸ **Amalur** *Priv.[20÷2]* €11 ℂ 696 241 175. c/Cerco Viejo.
❹ **Gares** *Priv. [40÷2]* €15 ℂ 722 198 134. ❺ **Puente** *Priv.[22÷3]* €15 +4 €40 ℂ 661 705 642 Paseo de los Fueros,57. ❻ **Estrella Guía** *Priv.[14÷3]* €15 +2 €40 ℂ 622 262 43 Paseo de Los Fueros, 34 / 2º piso. ❼ **Santiago Apostol** *Priv.*[100÷5]* €12 ℂ 948 340 220. ◖**Hoteles:** •*H* Bidean ℂ 948 341 156 c/Mayor from €50.
•*H* El Cerco ℂ 948 34 12 69 c/Rodrigo Ximenez de Rada from €45-60. •*Hs* **Zubi XXI** *x11* €30-€70 ℂ 948 340 921 c/ Irunbidea,28 •*Hs* **Plaza** *x8* €35-€50 ℂ 948 340 145, c/ Mayor, 52.
○ **Monumentos:** ❶ *Iglesia del Crucifijo* (Crucifijo XIV). ❷ *Iglesia de Santiago* (Peregrino Beltxa XII). ❸ *Iglesia San Pedro Apóstol* (N.S del Puy / Txori). ❹ *Puente la Reina* (Doña Mayor).

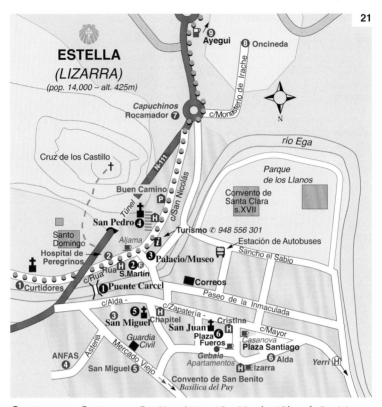

● **ESTELLA:** ❶ *Turismo:* ℂ 948 556 301 c/ San Nicolas / Plaza de San Martin.
◖**Albergues:** ❶ **Curtidores** *Priv.[30÷4]* €18 +4 €50 ℂ948 550 070 ❷ **Hospital Peregrinos** *Asoc.[80÷5]* €8 ℂ 948 550 200 c/La Rúa, 50. ❸ **Ágora** *Prv.[26÷3]* + €20 ℂ 948 546 574 c/Callizo Pelaires, 3 ❹ **ANFAS** *Mun.[24÷1]* €8 ℂ 639 011 688 c/Cordeleros, 7 Bajo. ❺ **San Miguel** *Par.[32÷2]* €-donativo ℂ 948 550 431 cMercado Viejo, 18 ❻ **Alda** *Priv.[12÷1]* €11 + €50 ℂ 948 030 137 *www. aldahotels.es* pl. Santiago ❼ **Rocamador** *Conv.[30÷7]*+ €16-20 +10 €40 ℂ 948 550 54 Hermanos Capuchinos c/ Rocamador 6 *(capilla virgen de Rocamador XII)*. ❽ *Juvenil* **Oncineda** *Muni.[150÷28]* €11 ℂ 948 555 022. ❾ **San Cipriano de Ayegui** *Mun.[80÷2]* ℂ 948 554 311 c/Polideportivo, Ayegui.

◖**Hostales:** •*Hospederia* **Convento Benedictinas** *x15* €35 Monasterio San Benito (Basilica del Puy). *c/San Nicolás:* •P*'*‍**Buen Camino** *x2* €40-50 ℂ 948 550 337 •*H* **Estella Rooms** *x15* €40-65 ℂ 848 850 000 *www.estellarooms.com*. •*Hs* **La Rúa** *x5* €80 ℂ 620 282 643 c/La Rua, 1. •*Hs´* **Cristina** *x13* €45-70 ℂ 948 550 450 c/Baja Navarre 1 / c/Mayor. •P*'*‍**Fonda Izarra** *x4* €20-40 ℂ 948 550 678 c/Caldería 20. •*P* •**Apartamentos Gebala** €50 ℂ 606 980 675 plaza Fueros, 31 •*H****‍* **Chapitel** *x14* €80+ ℂ 948 551 090 c/Chapitel, 1. *Otros:* •*Hs* **El Volante** *x11* €50+ ℂ 948 553 957 also •*Hs* **Area-99** ℂ 948 553 370. •*H**‍* **Yerri** *x28* €50+ ℂ 948 546 034.

○ **Monumentos:** ❶ *Puente de Carcel.* ❷ *Plaza San Martín Fuente de los Chorros XVI.* ❸ *Palacio de los Reyes de Navarra XII y museo.* ❹ *San Pedro de la Rúa y Claustro XII.* ❺ *Iglesia San Miguel.* ❻ *Iglesia de San Juan Bautista.*

05 PUENTE LA REINA – ESTELLA

⋯⋯	16.5 ⋯ ⋯75%
⋯⋯	5.4 ⋯ ⋯25%
⋯⋯	0.0
Total km	**21.9** km (*13.6 ml*)

Total ascent **300**m ± ½ *hr*
Alto ▲ Cirauqui **500**m (*1,640 ft*)
< 🅰 🅷 > ➲Mañeru **5.2**km ➲Cirauqui **7.8**km
➲Lorca **13.5**km ➲Villatuerta **18.0**km.

■ **Mañeru:** ●*Alb.***El Cantero** *Priv.[26÷3]* €11 ✆ 948 342 142 c/Esperanza. •*CR* **Isabel** ✆ 948 340 283. ■ **Cirauqui:** (*Zirauki*) 🍴 *El Portal*. Iglesia San Román *XIII* y *Santa Catalina*. ●*Alb.* **Par.**[*14÷1*] €-*donativo*. ●*Alb.***Maralotx** *Priv.[28÷3]*+2 €11 ✆ 678 635 208 *www.alberguecirauqui.com*.

■ **Lorca:** *Alb.*❶ **La Bodega del Camino** *Priv.[30÷5]*€13 +*3* €40 ✆ 948 541 327 c/Mayor opp: *Alb.*❷ **Lorca** *Priv.[12÷3]* €11 +*1* ✆ 948 541 190. 🍴 *Casa Julio* •*CR* **Nahia** *x5* €70+ ✆ 948 541 148 *www.casanahia.es*

■ **Villatuerta:** ●*Alb.* **Casa Mágica** *Priv.**[*21÷5*] €15 +*1* (menú €13) ✆ 948 732 313 *www.alberguelacasamagica.com* c/ Rebote, 5. ●*Alb.* **Etxeurdina** *Priv.[14÷2]* €15 ✆ 848 419 430 *www.etxeurdina.com* 🍴/•*CR* **643 km** *x4* €20-50 ✆ 615 003 090. *Iglesia de la Anunciación XIV (S. Veremundo)*

● **Estella** *p.21*

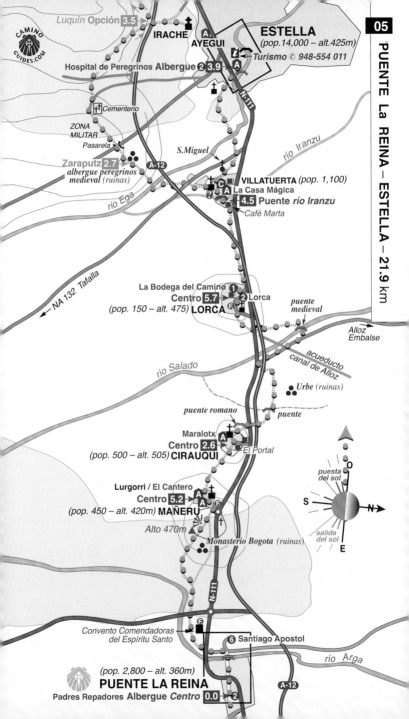

Luquín Opción **3.5**

IRACHE

A. AYEGUI

ESTELLA (pop. 14,000 – alt. 425m)
Turismo © 948-554 011

Hospital de Peregrinos Albergue **2** **3.9** A

Cementerio

ZONA MILITAR
Pasarela

Zaraputz **2.7**
albergue peregrinos medieval (ruinas)

río Ega

A-12

S.Miguel

río Iranzu

VILLATUERTA (pop. 1,100)
C A **La Casa Mágica**
4.5 **Puente río Iranzu**
Café Marta

NA 132 Tafalla

La Bodega del Camino
Centro **5.7** **1** **2** Lorca
(pop. 150 – alt. 475) **LORCA**

puente medieval

Alloz Embalse

río Salado

acueducto canal de Alloz

Urbe (ruinas)

puente romano   *puente*

Maralotx
Centro **2.6**
(pop. 500 – alt. 505) **CIRAUQUI**
El Portal

puesta del sol

O

S — N

E

salida del sol

Lurgorri / El Cantero
Centro **5.2** A A
(pop. 450 – alt. 420m) **MAÑERU**
Alto 470m

Monasterio Bogota (ruinas)

N-111

Convento Comendadoras del Espíritu Santo

6 Santiago Apostol

río Arga

(pop. 2,800 – alt. 360m)
PUENTE LA REINA
Padres Repadores Albergue *Centro* **0.0** **2**

A-12

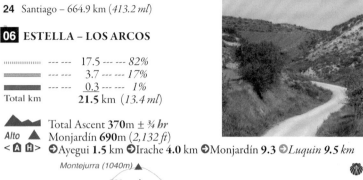

06 ESTELLA – LOS ARCOS

▪▪▪▪▪▪	--- ---	17.5	--- ---	*82%*
▬▬▬	--- ---	3.7	--- ---	*17%*
▬▬▬	--- ---	0.3	--- ---	*1%*
Total km		**21.5** km	(*13.4 ml*)	

Total Ascent **370**m ± ¾ *hr*

Alto ▲ Monjardín **690**m (*2,132 ft*)

< 🅰 🏠 > ➲Ayegui **1.5** km ➲Irache **4.0** km ➲Monjardín **9.3** ➲*Luquin 9.5 km*

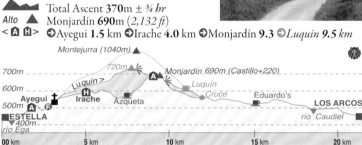

▪**Irache:** •**H**¨**Lur Gorri** *Irache* €50+ ✆ 948 558 286. ▲**Camping Irache** €30 -50 ✆948 555 555. ▪**Azqueta:** ●**Alb.** **La Perla Negra** *Priv.[5÷2]* €22 ✆627 114 797 c/Carrera,18. ▪**Villamayor:**❶ **Villamayor** *Priv.[20÷3]* €15 *+1* €40 ✆948 537 139. ❷ **Oasis Trails** *Asoc.[22÷4]* €11 *+1* €35 ✆623 428 216 *www. albergueoasistrails.com* •*CR* **Montedeio** €35-50 ✆ 948 551 521 c/ Mayor, 17 ●**Luquín** ●**Alb.** **Casa Tiago** Priv.*[14÷2]* €12 *+1* €30 ✆ 948 537 159

● **LOS ARCOS:** ❶ **la Fuente Casa de Austria** *Priv.[42÷3]* €12 *+5* €35 ✆ 948 640 797. ❷ **Casa de la Abuela** Priv.*[30÷3]* €15 *+3* €35 ✆ 948 640 250 adj. Plaza S. Maria. ❸ **Isaac Santiago** *Muni.[70÷8]* €8 ✆ 948 441 091 c/ El Hortal. ❹ **Casa Alberdi** *Priv.[24÷3]* €10 ✆ 948 640 764. •*P*'**Ostadar** *x6* €35+ ✆649 961 440 c/ San Lázaro 9. •*P***Mavi** *x5* €36+ ✆ 948 640 984 c/del Medio,7. •*H*¨**Mónaco** ✆948 640 000 €50+ Plaza del Coso. •*Hs* **Suetxe** *x8* €40 ✆ 948 441 175 c/Karramendabia opp. •*P* **Los Arcos** *x12* €40-70 ✆ José 608 585 153. •*H* **Villa de los Arcos** €55 ✆ 486 40 002. ❶ *Iglesia de Santa María XII.* ❷ *Portal de Castilla.* ❸ *Casa del Coso XVI* (❶ *Turismo*). ❹ *Ayuntamiento XVI.* ❺ *Portal del Dinero.*

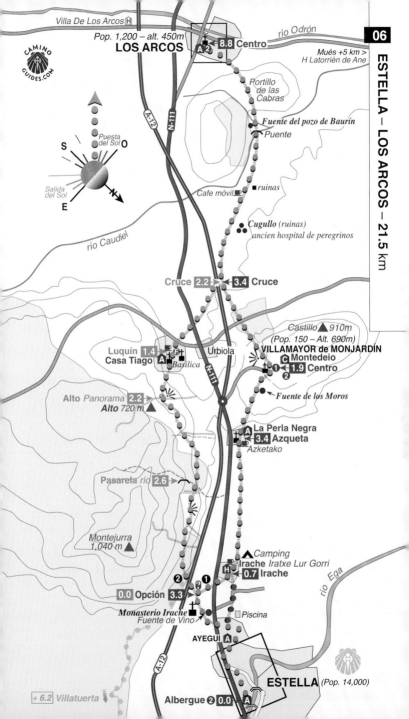

Villa De Los Arcos Ⓗ

río Odrón

Pop. 1,200 – alt. 450m
LOS ARCOS
Ⓐ **2** **8.8** **Centro**

Mués +5 km >
H Latorrién de Ane

Portillo de las Cabras

Fuente del pozo de Baurín
Puente

CAMINO
GUIDES.COM

S **O**
Puesta del Sol
Salida del Sol
E **N**

río Caudiel

Cafe móvil ▫▫ ■ *ruins*

Cugullo (ruinas)
ancien hospital de peregrinos

Cruce **2.2** ◀ **3.4** **Cruce**

Castillo ▲ *910m*
(Pop. 150 - Alt. 690m)
VILLAMAYOR de MONJARDÍN
Ⓒ **Montedeio**
1
† **2** **1.9** **Centro**

Luquín **1.4** †
Casa Tiago Ⓐ † *Basílica*
Urbiola

← *Fuente de los Moros*

Alto *Panorama* **2.2** ▲
Alto 720 m

Ⓐ **La Perla Negra**
† **3.4** **Azqueta**
Azketako

Pasarela *río* **2.6** →

Montejurra
1,040 m ▲

▲ *Camping*
Irache Iratxe Lur Gorri
Ⓗ **0.7** **Irache**

0.0 **Opción** **3.3**
2 **1**

Monasterio Irache ■
Fuente de Vino↗

▫ *Piscina*

AYEGUI Ⓐ

río Ega

✱ **ESTELLA** *(Pop. 14,000)*

+ 6.2 Villatuerta

Albergue 2 **0.0** Ⓐ

07 **LOS ARCOS – LOGROÑO**
Navarra   *La Rioja*

....	--- --- 18.4 --- --- 66%
▬▬▬	--- --- 8.3 --- --- 30%
▬▬	--- --- 1.1 --- --- 4%
Total km	**27.8** km (*17.3 ml*)

Total ascent **300**m ± ½ *hr*
Alto ▲ N. Sra. del Poyo **570**m (*1,870 ft*)
< 🅰 🏥 > ⊙Sansol **6.8**km ⊙Torres del Río **7.8**km ⊙Viana **18.4**km.

■ **Sansol:** ●*Alb.*Palacio *[32÷5]* €11-15 +€25-50 ✆ 617 641 852 Pl. del Sindicato.
●*Alb.* Sansol *Priv.[26÷1]* €10 / menú €8 ✆ 948 648 473 c/ Barrio Nuevo 4.
●*Alb.* Karma *Priv.[12÷2]* €6 ✆ 665 170 116 c/ Taconera, 11.●*CR* El Olivo *x5*
€25-50 ✆ 948 648 345. ●*Alb.* **Codés** *Priv .[24÷2]* ✆ 689 804 028 ⑪/🍴

■ **Torres del río:** •*Hs/Alb.* San Andrés *[20÷1]* €12 +*17* €45-65 ✆ 948 648 472
www.sanandreshostal.com. *Alb.*❶ Casa Mariela *Priv.***[70÷7]* €12 +*4* €30 ✆ 948
648 251 with ⑪/🍴 & shop. ❷la Pata & Oca *Priv.[32÷3]* €12 +5 €60 *www.*
alberguelapatadeoca.com + ⑪/🍴 c/ Mayor 5. ✝ *Iglesia de Santo Sepulcro XIIc* (€1).

● **VIANA:** ❶ *Turismo* ✆ 948 446 302. *Alb.*❶ Izar *Priv.[38÷4]* €10 +*2* €40 ✆
948 090 002. ❷ **Santa Maria** *Par.[17÷4]* €-donativo ✆ 948 645 037. ❸ Andrés
Muñoz *Mun.[46÷5]* €8 ✆ 948 645 530 c/San Pedro. •*P¨* San Pedro €30-40 ✆
948 645 927 c/Medio S.Pedro 13. •*H¨¨* Palacio de Pujadas *x28* €70+ ✆ 948
646 464 🖂 Portillo. •*Hs* Palacio Hernández *x6* €50-80 ✆ 639 222 986 *www.*
casapalaciohernandez.com

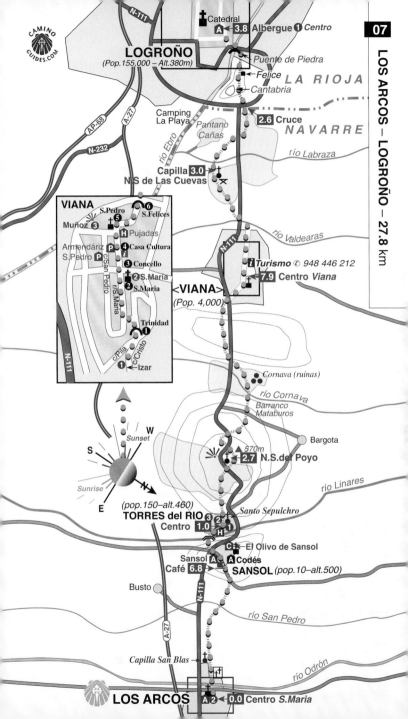

✝ Catedral
A ◄ 3.8 **Albergue** ❶ *Centro*

LOGROÑO
(Pop.155,000 – Alt.380m)

Puente de Piedra
Felice
Cantabria

LA RIOJA

Camping
La Playa
*Pantano
Cañas*

2.6 Cruce

NAVARRE

río Labraza

Capilla 3.0
N.S de Las Cuevas

río Valdearas

VIANA

S.Pedro ❻
Muñoz ❸ ❺ S.Felices
H Pujadas
Armendáriz P ❹ **Casa Cultura**
S.Pedro P *i*
c/San Pedro ❸ **Concello**
r/S.Maria ❷ **S.Maria**
❷ **S.Maria**

Trinidad ❶
c/Pila
c/Cristo ❶ ←Izar

i **Turismo** © 948 446 212
✝ ◄ **7.9** **Centro** *Viana*

◄VIANA►
(Pop. 4,000)

Cornava (ruinas)
río Cornava
*Barranco
Mataburos*

W
Sunset

S

Sunrise

E

▲570m
Bargota
✝ **2.7** **N.S.del Poyo**

río Linares

(pop. 150–alt.460)
TORRES del RIO ❸ ❷ ✝ *Santo Sepulchro*
Centro **1.0** H ❶

C ✝ **El Olivo de Sansol**
Sansol A ❿ A **Codés**
Café 6.8 **SANSOL** *(pop. 10–alt.500)*

Busto ○

río San Pedro

Capilla San Blas ✝

río Odrón

🐚 **LOS ARCOS** A ❷ ◄ **0.0** **Centro** *S.Maria*

LOGROÑO: ❶ *Turismo:* c/Portales,50 © 941 291 260.
○ *Monumentos:* **❶ Puente de Piedra**. **❷ Ermita San Gregorio y Casa de la Danza**. **❸ Iglesia y claustro Santa Maria del Palacio** *XII*. **❹ Iglesia San Bartolomé** *XIII*. **❺ Catedral de Santa María de la Redonda** *XIV (Las Gemelas).* **❻ Iglesia Santiago Real** *XVI*. **❼ Puerta del Camino** *Muralla del Revellín / Puerta Carlos.*

● *Albergues:* **◀Ruaviejo ❶** De Peregrinos de Logroño *Asoc.[65÷3]* €10 © 941 248 686 **❷** Santiago Apóstol *Priv.[78÷5]* €12 +3 €40 © 635 371 036 **❸** Santiago El Real *Par.[30+÷3]* €-donativo © 941 209 501 c/Barricocepo, 8 adj. Iglesia de Santiago. **❹** Logroño Bilbaina *Priv.[30÷8]* €15 +8 €36-€50 © 608 234 723. c/Capitán Gallarza, 10. **❺** Entresueños *Priv.[110÷14]* €10 +5 €40 © 941 271 334 c/ Portales, 12 adj. the cathedral. **❻** Winederful Hostel *[30÷4]* €20 © 678 495 109, c/ Herrerías, 2-14. **❼** Centro *[18÷3]* €10-18 © 678 495 109, Marqués de San Nicolás, 31. **❽**Albas *Priv.***[26÷1]* €15 © 688 766 Plaza Martínez Flamarique, 4 adj 🏠 *El Albero*.

● *Hostales: Centro:* •*H¨¨* F&G *x72* €52+ © 941 008 900 a/de Viana, 2-6. •*P* El Espolón *x4* €27+ © 601 021 200 c/San Juan •*P* Sotelo *x5* €27+ © 601 110 652 c/Calvo Sotelo, 18. •*H¨¨*M' de Vallejo *x47* €50 © 941 248 333 c/Marqués de Vallejo,8. •*Hs¨* La Numantina *x22* © 941 251 411 Sagasta, 4. •*H¨¨* Calle Mayor *x12* €80+ © 941 232 368 boutique hotel c/Marqués. •*H¨¨* Portales €80 © 941 502 794 c/ Portales, 85. ◀*Suburbs:* •*P* Parque Del Ebro *x4* €23 (pilgrim price) © 616 840 786 Paseo de La Constitución 24. •*P* Logroño *x5* €24+ © 941 101 186 c/Canalejas, 7. •*H¨¨*Murrieta *x104* €55+ © 941 224 150 Marqués de Murrieta, 1. •*H¨¨* Condes de Haro *x44* €71+ © 941 208 500 Saturnino Ulargui, 6. •*P* Saint Mateo *x6* €24+ © 620 637 191 c/Marqués de Murrieta, 35. ✣ *Planeta Agua 'trekking'* Av. de Navarra,8 © 941-252 764. ✣ *Lavanderia S.Mateo* c/Doce,4 (08:00-22:00). 🍴 *Tapas* *c/ Laurel* + *c/San Juan*.

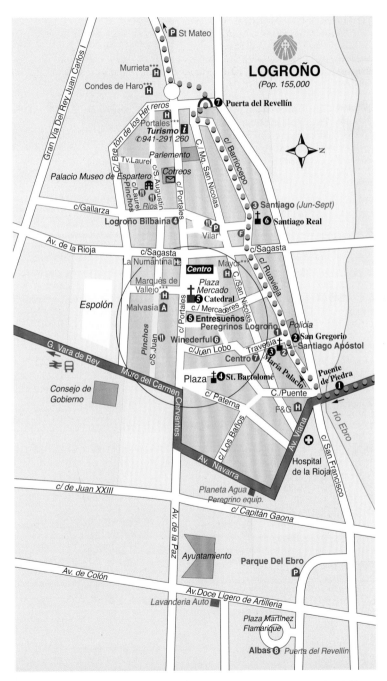

08 LOGROÑO – NÁJERA

‧‧‧‧‧‧‧‧‧‧	--- --- 23.1 --- ---	*80%*
———	--- --- 3.8 --- ---	*13%*
———	--- --- 2.0 --- ---	*7%*
Total km	**28.9** km	*(18.0 ml)*

Total ascent **300**m ± *½ hr*
Alto Poyo Roldán **600**m *(1,968 ft)*
< 🅰 🄷 > ⊙Navarrete **12.7** km
⊙*Ventosa* **18.4** km *(+1.4 km)*

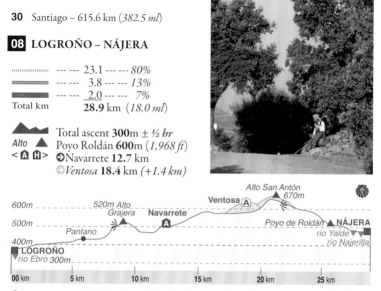

● **Navarrete:** ●*Alb.* El Camino de las Estrellas *Priv.[40÷3]* €12 *+4* €40 ✆ 623 220 746. ❶ Casa del Peregrino Angel *Priv.[18÷1]* €12 *+1* €35 ✆ 630 982 928 c/ Cruz. ❷ Navarrete Centro *Asoc.[34÷3]* €10 ✆ 941 440 722. ❸ Buen Camino *Priv.[6÷1]* €12 *+2* €35 ✆ 941 440 318 *(Hs Villa c/ Cruz)*. ❹ La Iglesia *Priv.[15÷3]*€15 ✆ 602 265 787 c/Mayor Alta, 2. ❺ El Cántaro *Priv.[17÷2]* €12 +5 €35 ✆ 941 441 180 c/Herrerías. ❻ A la Sombra del Laurel *Priv.[14÷2]* €15 *+6* €30-50 ✆ 639 861 110 Carretera de Burgos, 52. ◖ **Hotels:** •*Hs* Villa de Navarrete *x8* €30 ✆ 941 440 318 c/La Cruz. •*H⁺⁺* Rey Sancho *x12* €65+ ✆ 941 441 378 c/Mayor Alta + •*P⁺* Peregrinando *x5* €55+ ✆ 622 164 328. •*P* Posada Ignatius *x9* €55 ✆ 941 124 094, Pl. Arco, 4. •*H⁺⁺* San Camilo *x38* €50+ ✆ 941 441 111 northern bypass.● ● ● *Sotés:* (+1.5 km) •*CR* San Martín €15 ✆ 941 441 768 c/ S.Miguel, 67.● ● ●*Ventosa:* *Alb* ♥ San Saturnino *Priv.*⁺*[42÷6]* €13 ✆ 941 441 899. •*H⁺⁺* Las Águedas *x7* €55-75 ✆ 941 441 774 Plaza S. Coloma.

● **NÁJERA:** ●*Alb.* El Peregrino *Priv* c/ San Fernando 90. ❶ *Turismo* ✆ 941 360 041 Estacion de bus. ❶ Puerta de Nájera *Priv.[29÷9]* €15-20 *+3* €40 c/ Carmen ✆ 941 362 317. ❷ Nido de Cigüeña *Priv.[15÷5]* €15 Tania ✆ 611 095 191 Calleja Cuarta San Miguel,4. ❸ Nájera *Asoc[50÷1]* €-donativo. ❹ Sancho III *Priv.[16÷4]* €12 *+4* €30 ✆ 941 361 138 + *La Judería* menú €8. ❺Las Peñas *Priv.[10÷3]* €10 *+1* €30 ✆ 621 209 432 c/ Costanilla 56. ◖*Hostales:* •*P* San Lorenzo *x6* €35 c/ Garrán 10 + •*P* S.Lorenzo 2 c/ Primera San Miguel, 6 ✆ 941 363 722 •*Hs⁺⁺* Ciudad de Nájera €45+ Aitor ✆ 941 360 660 c/ San Miguel, 14. •*H⁺⁺⁺* Duques de Nájera €60+ ✆ 941 410 421 c/ Carmen, 7 •*Hs⁺* Hispano €36-50 ✆ 941 363 615 c/La Cepa,2.

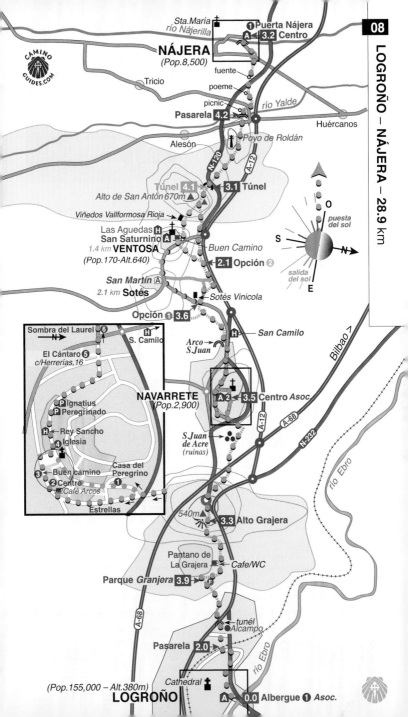

Sta.María
río Nájerilla
① Puerta Nájera
Ⓐ **3.2 Centro**

NÁJERA
(Pop.8,500)

Tricio

fuente
poeme
picnic
Pasarela 4.2

río Yalde

Huércanos

Alesón
Poyo de Roldán

① Túnel 4.1
Alto de San Antón 670m ▲
3.1 Túnel

Viñedos Vallformosa Rioja

Ⓗ
Las Aguedas Ⓐ
San Saturnino
1.4 km **VENTOSA**
(Pop.170-Alt.640)

Buen Camino
2.1 Opción ②

San Martín Ⓐ
2.1 km **Sotés**

Sotés Vinícola

Opción ① **3.6**

Ⓗ
San Camilo

Arco →
S.Juan

Sombra del Laurel ⑥
S. Camilo Ⓗ
El Cántaro ⑤
c/Herrerías,16

NAVARRETE
(Pop.2,900)

Ⓟ Ignatius
Ⓟ Peregrinado
Ⓗ Rey Sancho
④ Iglesia

③ Buen camino
② Centro
Café Arcos

Casa del
Peregrino ①

Estrellas

Ⓐ ② **3.5 Centro** *Asoc.*

*S.Juan
de Acre
(ruinas)*

540m **3.3 Alto Grajera**

Pantano de
La Grajera
Cafe/WC

Parque *Granjera* **3.9**

tunél
Alcampo

Pasarela 2.0

(Pop.155,000 – Alt.380m)
Cathedral
LOGROÑO
Ⓐ **0.0 Albergue ①** *Asoc.*

O
*puesta
del sol*
S
N
*salida
del sol*
E

Bilbao ↗
A-12
N-232
A-68
río Ebro
N-120

09 NÁJERA – SANTO DOMINGO de la CALZADA

╌╌╌╌╌	--- --- 15.1 --- --- *71%*
▬▬▬	--- --- 5.0 --- --- *23%*
▬▬	--- --- 1.2 --- --- *6%*
Total km	**21.3** km (*13.2 ml*)

Total ascent **300m ± ½ hr**
Alto ▲ Cirueña **745**m (*2,444 ft*)
<▲ ⊞> ➲Azofra **6.1**km ➲Cirueña **15.5** km

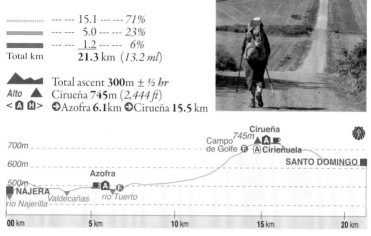

■ **Azofra:** *Alb.*❶ Azofra *Muni.[60÷30]* €10 ⓒ 941 379 325 c/Las Parras (+200m). ❷ **Herbert Simón** *Par.[26÷2]* ⓒ 607 383 811 adj. *N.S. de los Ángeles.* •*P* **La Plaza** *x4* €30-45 ⓒ 941 379 239 Pl. de España 7. •*H*¨**Real Casona de las Amas** *x16* ⓒ 941 416 103 c/Mayor. ● *Cañas: Abadía Cisterciense de Cañas XII.* •*Hs* **La Casona** ⓒ 941-379 150. •*Hs* **La Posada del Santo** ⓒ 941-204 187.
■ **Cirueña:** ❶ **Virgen de Guadalupe** *Priv.**[10÷5] €15 ⓒ 638 924 069 c/ Barrio Alto. ❷ **Victoria** *Priv.**[10÷2] €14 +2 €40 ⓒ 941 426 105 c/S.Andres. •*P*`**Casa Victoria** *x4* €30+ ⓒ 941 426 105 adj. ☛ *Jacobeo.*

● **SANTO DOMINGO de la Calzada:** ❶ *Turismo* ⓒ 941 341 238 c/Mayor, 33 (10:00–14:00 / 16:00–19:00). *Alb.*❶ **Abadía Cisterciences** *Conv.[32÷4]* €9 941 340 700 c/Mayor 29-31. ❷ **Casa de la Cofradía del Santo** *Asoc.[185÷10]* €11 ⓒ 941 343 390 www.alberguecofradiadelsanto.com. ◖*Hostales:* •*Hs*¨ **Hospedería Cistercienses** *(Santa Teresita)* €40+ ⓒ 941 340 700 modern hostel run by the Cistercian nuns c/Pinar, 2. •*H*¨¨**El Corregidor** €40+ ⓒ 941 342 128 c/Mayor,14. •*Hs*`**Rey Pedro I** *x9* €50+ ⓒ 941 341 160 c/S.Roque, 9. •*Hs* **La Catedral** €45+ ⓒ 651 948 260 c/ Isidoro Salas. •*P*`**Miguel** €25+ ⓒ 941 343 252 c/Juan Carlos I, 23. •*Hs*`**El Molino de Floren** €40 ⓒ 941 342 031 c/Margubete. •*H*¨¨¨**Parador de Santo Domingo** €85+ ⓒ 941 340 300 Plaza del Santo. •*H*¨¨¨ **Parador Bernardo de Fresneda** €90+ ⓒ 941 341 150. •*Hs* **Room Concept** *x10* €30+ ⓒ 941 342 366 c/ Alberto Etchegoyen, 2. •*Hs* **Carpe Viam** *x6* €37+ ⓒ 661 883 195 c/ Isidoro Salas, 58. •*Hs* **Atuvera**¨¨ *x6* €40+ ⓒ 941 445 318 c/ Mayor, 6.

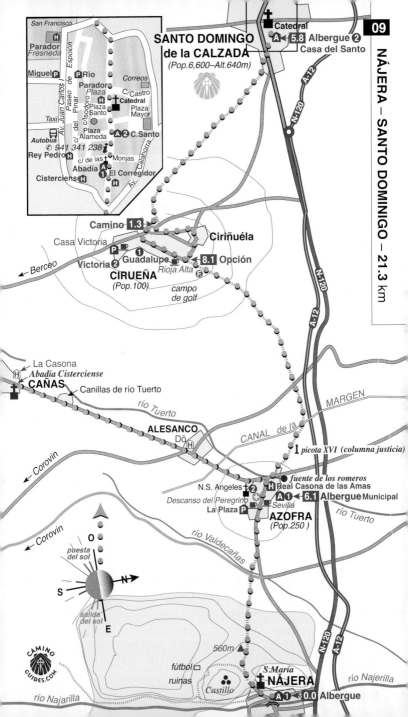

SANTO DOMINGO de la CALZADA
(Pop.6,600–Alt.640m)

† Catedral

A ◄ 5.8 Albergue 2
Casa del Santo

San Francisco

H Parador Fresneda

Miguel P

Río

P Río
Parador Plaza
Correos
C/Castro
† Catedral
Plaza Santo
H
Plaza Mayor
Plaza Alameda

Taxi

Autobus
© 941 341 238 *i*
Rey Pedro

A 2 C.Santo

c/ de las † Monjas
A
1 El Corregidor

Cistercienses H
H

Camino 1.3 ►

Ciriñuéla

Casa Victoria

P
1
Victoria 2 Guadalupe
Rioja Alta
8.1 Opción

CIRUEÑA
(Pop.100)

campo de golf

F

Berceo ←

La Casona
Abadia Cisterciense
H
† CAÑAS
Canillas de río Tuerto

río Tuerto

MARGEN

ALESANCO
Dô
H

CANAL de la

picota XVI *(columna justicia)*

Corovin ←

fuente de los romeros
N.S. Angeles † 2
H Real Casona de las Amas
A 1 ◄ 6.1 Albergue Municipal

Descanso del Peregrino
Sevilla
La Plaza P
AZOFRA
(Pop.250)
río Tuerto

Corovin ←

río Valdecañas

O
puesta del sol
N
S
salida del sol
E

CAMINO
GUIDES.COM

560m ▲
fútbol □
ruinas
Castillo

S.María
† NÁJERA
A 1 ◄ 0.0 Albergue

río Najerilla

río Najarilla

10 SANTO DOMINGO – BELORADO

‖‖‖‖‖‖	--- --- 16.2 --- ---	72%
══════	--- --- 5.4 --- ---	24%
▬▬▬▬	--- --- 0.8	4%
Total km	22.4 km (*13.9 ml*)	

Total ascent **300**m ± ½ *hr*
Alto ▲ Villamayor del Río **810**m (*2,657 ft*)
< **A H** > ➲ Grañón **6.7**km ◌ *Carrasquedo* **7.9**km(+*1.2 km*) ➲ Redecilla **10.5**km
➲ Castildelgado **12.2**km ➲ Viloria de la Rioja **14.1** ➲ Villamayor del Río **17.5** km

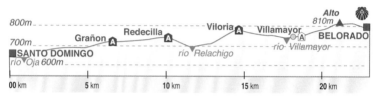

■ **Grañón:** *Alb.*❶ S.Juan Bautista *Par.[40÷2]* €-donativo + cena comunitaria ✆
941 420 818. ◀**c/ Mayor ❷** La Casa de las Sonrisas *Priv*. *[27÷7]* ✆ 687 877
891 €-donativo. •*CR* Jacobea *x3* ✆ 941 420 684 c/Mayor Nº32. •*CR* Cerro de
Mirabel *x4* Nº40 ✆ 660 166 090. •*P* El Cuartel *x9* €20+ ✆ 627 341 907. •*H*ʺʺ
Casa Grande *x11* €130 ✆ 941 457 726.

■ **Redecilla del Camino: c/ Mayor** *Alb.*❶ Essentia *Priv.[10÷2]* €12 ✆ 606 046
298. ❷ San Lázaro *Muni.[52÷4]* €5 ✆ 947 585 221.•*H* Redecilla *x7* €30 ✆
947 585 256. ■ **Castildelgado:** ●*Alb.* Bideluze *Priv.[16÷3]*+ €11 +€35 ✆ 616
647 115 c/ Mayor, 8. ‖/*Hs*ʺ El Chocalatero *x37* € 25+ ✆ 947 588 063 ■ **Viloria
de la Rioja** *Alb.*❶ Parada Viloria *Priv.[16÷3]* €8 ✆ 639 451 660 c/Bajera, 37.
❷Acacio & Orietta *Priv.[10÷1] V*. €8 ✆ 947 585 220 c/ Nueva. •*MiHotelito x7*
€70+ ✆ 947 585 225 Plaza Mayor, 16. ● *Villamayor del Río* (+*0.3 km*): ●*Alb.*
San Luis de Francia *Priv.**[*26÷6]* €5 / menú €8 ✆ 947 580 566. ● *Quintanilla
del Monte:* •*CR* La Encantada €50 ✆ 947 580 484.

● **BELORADO:** ❶ *Turismo centro Jacobea* (10:30-20:00) ✆ 941 341 238 Plaza
Mayor. *Alb.*❶ A Santiago *Priv.**[*98÷8]* €10-15 ✆ 947 562 164. ❷ Santa María
Par.[20÷4] €-donativo ✆ 947 580 085. ❸ El Corro *Muni.[45÷4]* €8 ✆ 947
581 419 c/ Mayor, 68. ❹ El Caminante *Priv.**[*22÷1]* €10 +8 €35 ✆ 947 580
231. ❺ Punto B *Priv.[8÷1]* €15 +*16* €48+ ✆ 947 580 591 [www.hostelpuntob.](www.hostelpuntob.com)
[com](www.hostelpuntob.com) c/Cuatro Cantones, 4. ❻ Cuatro Cantones *Priv.[65÷6]* €12-16 ✆ 947 580
591 www.cuatrocantones.com c/Hipólito Lopez Bernal. + **0.7 km** •*P/Alb.*El Salto
Fernando ✆ 947 614 324 www.elsalto.eu eco hostel c/ Camino los Cauces.

◀*Hoteles:* •*H* La Huella *x8* €35-50 ✆ 947 564 748 c/Mayor 49. •*CR* Waslala ♥
x3 (oasis of peace & harmony) €25 full board €45 ✆ 947 580 726 c/Mayor 57. •*P*
Toni *x5* €35-45 ✆ 947 580 525 c/Redecilla del Campo adj.*Correos*. •*H*Jacobeo
x16 €55+ ✆ 947 580 010 on the main road or at the end of town •*H* Belorado
x11 €35-50 ✆ 947 580 684.

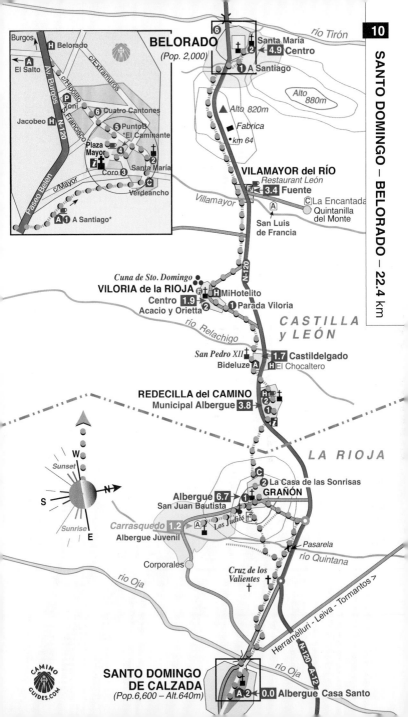

río Tirón

Burgos
H Belorado
A El Salto
Av. Burgos
c/Hipolito
c/Extramuros

BELORADO
(Pop. 2,000)

6
† 2 Santa Maria
4.9 Centro

1 A Santiago

Alto 880m

P Toni
Jacobeo H
N-120
c/Francisco

6 Cuatro Cantones
5 PuntoB
*El Caminante
Plaza Mayor
4
i †
Coro 3
Santa María
Verdeancho
c/Mayor
C

Paseo Belén

A 1 A Santiago*

▲ Alto 820m
■ Fabrica
• km 64

VILAMAYOR del RÍO
Restaurant León
F **3.4** Fuente
C La Encantada
Quintanilla
del Monte
A

Villamayor

San Luis
de Francia

N-120

Cuna de Sto. Domingo
VILORIA de la RIOJA
† H MiHotelito
Centro **1.9**
2
1 Parada Viloria
Acacio y Orietta

CASTILLA
y LEÓN

río Relachigo

San Pedro XII †
A **1.7** Castildelgado
Bideluze
H El Chocaltero

REDECILLA del CAMINO
Municipal Albergue **3.8**
H 2 †
1
i

LA RIOJA

N
W
Sunset
S
E
Sunrise

C 2 La Casa de las Sonrisas
GRAÑÓN
Albergue **6.7** 1
San Juan Bautista †
Carrasquedo **1.2** A 2 Los Judíos
Albergue Juvenil ■

Corporales

Cruz de los Valientes †

Pasarela
río Quintana

río Oja

Herramélluri – Leiva – Tormantos >

N-120 A-12

río Oja

SANTO DOMINGO
DE CALZADA
(Pop.6,600 – Alt.640m)
† A 2 **0.0** Albergue Casa Santo

CAMINO GUIDES.COM

11 BELORADO – SAN JUAN de ORTEGA

,,,,,,,,,,,,,,,,	--- --- 22.5 --- ---	*93%*
═══════	--- --- 1.5 --- ---	*6%*
▬▬▬▬	--- --- 0.2 --- ---	*1%*
Total km	**24.2** km	(*15.0 ml*)

Total ascent **500**m ± ¾ *hr*
Alto ▲ Montes de Oca: **1,150**m (*3,773 ft*)
< 🅰 🅗 > ❍Tosantos **4.8**km ❍Villambistia **6.8**km
❍Epinosa del Camino **8.4** ❍Villafranca **12.0** km

[elevation profile]
1,100m ····· Alto Mojapán ····· Alto Pedraja **1,100**m
1,000m ····· [!] ····· **SAN JUAN**
····· *arroyo Peroja* ·····
900m ····· **Villafranca** 🅰
Espinosa 🅰 *río Oca*
Villambistia 🅰
800m **Tosantos** 🅰
▬**BELORADO**
río Tirón **700**m
00 km   5 km   10 km   15 km   20 km

▌**Tosantos:** *Alb.* ❶ S. Francisco de Asís *Par.[30÷3]* €-*donativo* + *cena comunitaria* ℂ 947 580 371. ❷ **Los Arancones** *Priv.[16÷1]* €10 ℂ 947 581 485 c/ de la Iglesia. 🍴 *El Castaño.* ▌**Villambistia:** ●*Alb.*San Roque *Muni.* *[12÷1]* €10 ℂ 680 501 887 (+200m). •*CR* los Deseos *x6*€35 ℂ 947 108 588. ▌**Espinosa del camino:** ❶ La Cantina(Taberna) *Priv.* *[18÷3]* €10 ℂ 947 570 430, c/ Barruelo. ❷ **La Campana** *Priv.[10÷2]* €17 *incl.* ℂ 678 479 361. •**Casa Las Almas** *[5÷2]* €12 ℂ 618 568 845. ▌**Villafranca de Montes de Oca:** *Alb.* ❶ **Villafranca** *Mun.[60÷4]* €5-7 ℂ 691 801 211. ❷ **San Antón Abad** *Priv*.[49÷3]* €15 *+3* €40+ ℂ 947 582 150. •*Hs¨¨*San Antón Abad *x14* €70 ℂ 947 582 151. •*CR* **La Alpargatería** *x6* €25-45 *www.casaruralalpargateria.es* ℂ 686 040 884 adj' •*Hs* El Pajaro €25 ℂ 947 582 029 •*P* Jomer *x8* €35-55 ℂ 947 582 146

● **San Juan de Ortega:** ●*Alb.* San Juan *Par.[60÷3]* €15 *incl* ℂ 947 560 438 *www.alberguesanjuandeortega.es.* •*CR* La Henera *x10* €47-€55 ℂ 606 198 734 *www.sanjuandeortega.es.* ●*Alb* El descanso de San Juan *Priv.* *[7÷1]* €15 *+2* José Luis ℂ 690 398 024. *Iglesia de San Nicolás de Barri XV.*

Montes de Oca
Monumento de los Caídos

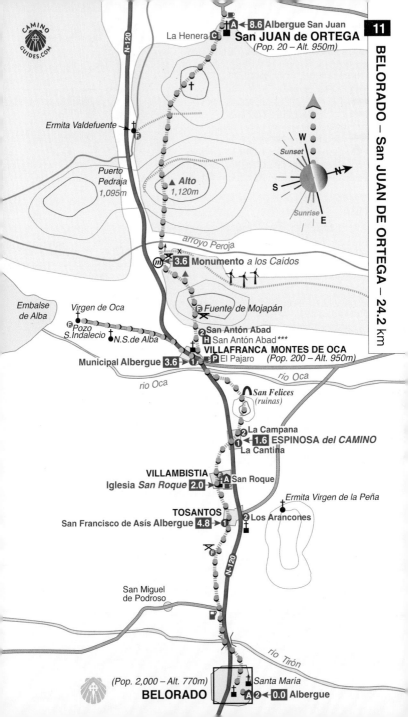

CAMINO
GUIDES.com

†A ◄ **8.6** Albergue San Juan
La Henera C **San JUAN de ORTEGA**
(Pop. 20 – Alt. 950m)

†

Ermita Valdefuente † F

Puerto
Pedraja
1,095m

▲ **Alto**
1,120m

W
Sunset
N
S
E
Sunrise

arroyo Peroja

m **3.6** ► **Monumento** *a los Caídos*

Embalse
de Alba

Virgen de Oca †
F **Fuente de Mojapán**

F Pozo
S.Indalecio †
N.S. de Alba

2 **San Antón Abad**
H San Antón Abad ***
VILLAFRANCA MONTES DE OCA ***
(Pop. 200 – Alt. 950m)

Municipal Albergue 3.6 ► 1 P El Pajaro

río Oca
río Oca

∩ **San Felices**
(ruinas)

2 **La Campana**
1 ◄ **1.6** **ESPINOSA** *del CAMINO*
La Cantina

VILLAMBISTIA
Iglesia *San Roque* **2.0** A San Roque

Ermita Virgen de la Peña †

TOSANTOS
San Francisco de Asís Albergue **4.8** ► 1 2 **Los Arancones**
†

F

San Miguel
de Podroso

N-120

río Tirón

(Pop. 2,000 – Alt. 770m)

† **Santa María**
BELORADO A 2 ◄ **0.0** Albergue

12 SAN JUAN de ORTEGA – BURGOS

....	--- --- 17.7 --- --- *68%*	
▬▬▬▬▬	--- --- 4.4 --- --- *17%*	
▬▬▬▬▬	--- --- <u>4.0</u> --- --- *15%*	
Total km	**26.1** km (*16.2 ml*)	

Total ascent **200**m ± ¼ *hr*

Alto ▲ Sierra Atapuerca **1,080**m (*3,543 ft*)

< 🅰 🅷 > ➲Agés **3.6** km ➲Atapuerca **6.1**km
➲*Olmos* **8.5***km* ➲Cardeñuela **12.4**km ➲Orbaneja **14.5**km ➲Castañares **19.1**km.

Profile:
SAN JUAN — Agés — Alto 1,080m Cruz de Matagrande — Atapuerca — río Vena — Obaneja **C** — Castañares **H** — BURGOS 850m — río Arlanzón
1,000m / 900m / 800m — 00 km — 5 km — 10 km — 15 km — 20 km — 25

● **Santovenia De Oca / N-120** (+3.9 km) ●*Alb.* **El Camino** *Priv.[24÷2]* €12 ©
650 733 150. •*H¨* **Sierra de Atapuerca** €40 © 947 106 912 ▮ **Agés:** ●*Alb* **El Pajar**
Priv.*[24÷4] €14 +2 €45 ©686 273 322 *menú.* ●*Alb* **La Taberna** *Muni.[36÷1]*
€8-10 © 947 400 697 🍴 *menú.* ●*Alb* **Fagus** *[22÷5]*+ €12 © 947 561 329.

▮ **Atapuerca:** *Alb.*❶ **El Peregrino** *Priv.[30÷6]* €11 + €40 © 661 580 882
<u>www.alberguatapuerca.com</u>. *Alb.*❷ **La Hutte** *Priv.[18÷1]* €10 © 947 430 320
(+300m). *Alb.*❸ **La Plazuela Verde** *Priv.[10÷1]* €14© 658 647 720 •*H¨* **Papasol**
x6 €56 ©947 430 320. •*Hs* **El Palomar** *x5* €60 © 947 430 549 + 🍴 c/ Revilla. •*CR*
El Pesebre *x5* €45-55 © 610 564 147 c/Iglesia. ● *Olmos de Atapuerca:* (+2.4
km) ●*Alb.* **Olmos** *Muni.[21÷3]* €10 © 633 586 876 + 🍴 *Meson los Hidalgos menú.*
•*CR* **La Serrezuela** *x3* €60 © 635 313 055. •*CR* **Los Olmos** *x5* €50+ © 645 109
032. ▮ **Cardeñuela Riopico:** *Alb.*❶ **Vía Minera** *Priv.[38÷5]* €8 +2 €50 c/ La
Iglesia © 652 941 647 (+200m) *menú.* ❷ **Cardeñuela** *Muni.[12÷2]* €7 © 646
249 597 + 🍴 *La Parada.* ❸ **Santa Fe** *Priv. [15÷2]* €12 +3 €40 +*menú* © 626
352 269 <u>www.baralberguesantafe.com</u> •*CR* **La Cardeñuela** *x3* €25 © 947 210 479.
▮ **Orbaneja** 🍴 *El Peregrino.* •*CR* **Fortaleza** *x6* €50 © 947 225 354

❶● **Castañares N-120:**•*H¨* **Asador** *x14* €55 ©947 474 977.
❷● **Villafría:** •*H¨* **Iruñako** *x31* €38-50 © 947 484 126. •*H¨* **Buenos Aires** *x87*
€40-50 © 947 483 740. •*H¨* **Las Vegas** *x82* €35-50 © 947 484 453.
❸● **Parque Fluvial***: Cartuja de Miraflores* <u>www.cartuja.org</u>. •*Camping.* **Fuente**
Blancas Bungalow €40 © 947 486 016.

❸● *Parque Fluvial*

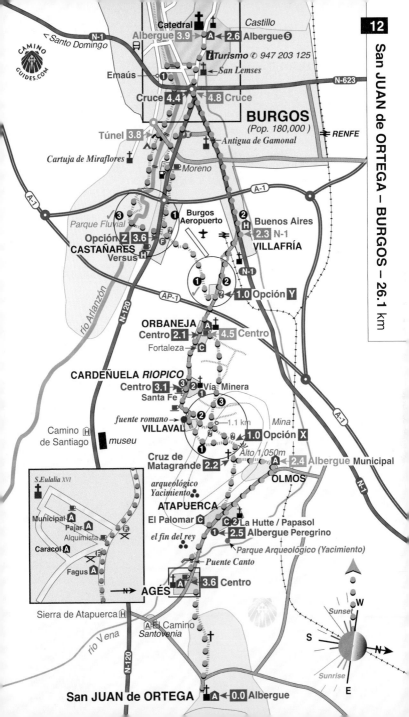

Catedral

Albergue **3.9** A **2.6** Albergue **5**

Castillo

i Turismo © 947 203 125

San Lemses

Emaús

Cruce **4.4** ← **4.8** Cruce

N-623

BURGOS
(Pop. 180,000)

⇐ RENFE

Túnel **3.8**

Antigua de Gamonal

Cartuja de Miraflores †

Moreno

A-1

3
Parque Fluvial

Burgos Aeropuerto

2 Buenos Aires
H
2.3 N-1

Opción **Z** **3.6**

VILLAFRÍA

CASTAÑARES
Versus

N-1

AP-1

1 **2**

1.0 Opción **Y**

N-120

rio Arlanzón

ORBANEJA

Centro **2.1** → A ← **4.5** Centro

Fortaleza — C

CARDEÑUELA *RIOPICO*

Centro **3.1** → **2** Vía-Minera

Santa Fe **1** **3**

fuente romano → **2**
VILLAVAL ← 1.1 km

Mina

1 **1.0** Opción **X**

Camino 🏠
de Santiago ■ *museu*

Alto 1,050m
A **2.4** Albergue Municipal

Cruz de
Matagrande **2.2**

OLMOS

*arqueológico
Yacimiento*

ATAPUERCA

El Palomar C

C **2** La Hutte / Papasol
1 **2.5** Albergue Peregrino

el fin del rey

Parque Arqueológico (Yacimiento)

Puente Canto

A ■ **3.6** Centro

S.Eulalia XVI †

Municipal A
Pajar A
Alquimista ■ ✗
Caracol A
Fagus A

→ **AGÉS**

N

W
Sunset

S

N

Sierra de Atapuerca 🏠

A El Camino
Santovenia

E

Sunrise

rio Vena

N-120

San JUAN de ORTEGA   A ← **0.0** Albergue

●*Albergues:* ❶ **Casa de Peregrinos Emaús** *Par.[10÷4]* €10 C/ de San Pedro de Cardeña. ❷ **Hostel Burgos** *Priv.[68÷11]* Ⓒ 947 250 801 c/ Miranda, 4. ❸ **Santiago y Santa Catalina** *[16÷1]* €10 Ⓒ947 207 952, c/ Laín Calvo, 10. . ❹ **Catedral Burgos** *[136÷23]* €22 incl. (+90) Ⓒ 947 718 435. ❺ **La Casa del Cubo** *Lerma Asoc.[150÷6]* €10 Ⓒ 947 460 922, c/Fernán González, 28.

● *Hostales Centro:* *Plaza S. Lemses* (c/Cardenal Benlloch) •*P* **Santiago** *x9* €36+ Ⓒ 947 046 230. •*Hs¨* **Lar** *x11* €25+ Ⓒ 947 209 655. •*Hs* **Boreal** *x17* €50+ Ⓒ 947 205 134. •*Hsr¨* **Carrales** *x10* €20+ Ⓒ 947 263 547 c/ Puente Gasset,4. •*Hsr¨* **Manjón** *x10* €27 Ⓒ 947 208 689 c/Gran Teatro adj. •*H¨¨¨* **Almirante Bonifaz** Ⓒ 947 206 943. ◖ *Barrio antigua:* •*H¨¨* **La Puebla** Ⓒ 947 203 350 c/La Puebla Nº4 + Nº6 •*Hr¨* **Cordón** *x35* Ⓒ 947 265 000. •*Hr˙* **El Jacobeo** Ⓒ 947 260 102 c/ San Juan •*Hr¨¨* **Centro Los Braseros** Ⓒ 947 252 958. •*Hsr¨* **Norte y Londres** Ⓒ 947 264 125. ◖ *Central c/Fernán Gonzaléz* €65+: •*H¨¨¨* **Palacio de los Blasones** Ⓒ 947 271 000 @Nº10 (*pilgrim discount*). •*H¨¨¨* **Mesón del Cid / Cid II** *x49* €75+ Ⓒ 947 208 715 @Nº62. •*H¨¨¨* **Abba Burgos** *x99* Ⓒ 947 001 100 @ Nº72 (antiguo Seminario). ◖ *Rio:* •*H* **Urban Burgos** *x7* Ⓒ 644 735 999 c/Miranda, 12 (adj. estación de autobuses). •*H¨¨* **Via Gotica** Ⓒ 947 244 444 Plaza de Vega. •*H¨¨¨* **NH Palacio de la Merced** €75+ Ⓒ 947 479 900 c/Merced.

○ **Monumentos históricos:** ❶ *San Lesmes* *XIV & Mo. S. Juan* (*mueso Marceliano*) ❷ *Arco S. Juan* *XIII* ❸ *Casa del Cordón* *XV* ❹ *San Gil* *XIV* ❺ *S. Esteban* *XIV* (*mueso Retablo*) ❻ *S. Nicolas de Barri* *XV* ❼ *Catedral de Santa María* *XIII* (9:30-18:30) €7 (+ credencial €3.50). ❽ *Arco & Puente de Santa María* *XIV* ❾ *Solar del Cid* ❿ *Arco S.Martin* *XIII.* ⓫ *Santa María la Real de Las Huelgas* *XII* (*museo*). ⓬ *Hospital del Rey* *XII* (*antiguo hospital del peregrino*). ● *Cartuja de Miraflores* *XV* (+4 *km*). ● *Museo de la Evolución de Humana* Paseo Sierra de Atapuerca (10:00-14:30 / 16:30-20:00) €6.

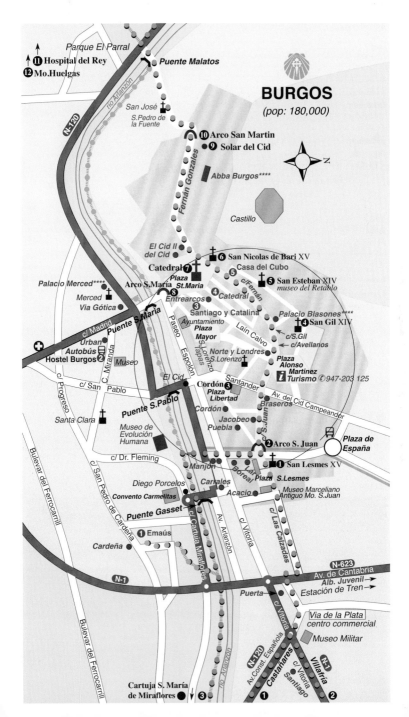

13 BURGOS – HORNILLOS del CAMINO

....	--- --- 14.0 --- ---	67%
▬▬▬	--- --- 3.2 --- ---	15%
▬▬▬	--- --- 3.8 --- ---	18%
Total km	**21.0** km (*13.0 ml*)	

Total ascent **150**m ± ¼ *hr*

Alto ▲ Meseta **950**m (*3,117 ft*)

< Ⓐ Ⓗ > ➲N-120 Burgos **2.2** km ➲Tarjados **10.6** km
➲Rabé de las Calzadas **13.0** km.

Alto (Meseta)
950m

900m
BURGOS   **Tarjados**   **Rabé**   **HORNILLOS**
800m   *rio Urbel*   825m
rio Arlanzón   *rio Arlanzón*

00 km   5 km   10 km   15 km   20 km

▮ **Burgos N-620 and N-120:** •*H¨* **Puerta Romeros** Ⓒ 947 460 738. •*Hs¨¨* **Abadía Camino Santiago** *x29* €40 Ⓒ 947 040 404 and •*Hs¨* **Via Láctea** Ⓒ 947 463 211.
▮ **Tardajos:** *Alb.* ❶ **La Fábrica** *Priv.[14÷4]* €12 *+6* €50 Ⓒ 620 111 939 *www.alberguelafabrica.com* c/La Fábrica + *menú.* ❷ **La Casa de Beli** *Priv.[34÷5]* €10 *+7* €45+ Ⓒ 947 451 234 *www.lacasadebeli.com* ❸ **Tardajos** *Muni.[18÷3]* €-*donativo* Ⓒ 947 451 189 adj. ☛ *El Camino.* •*P* **Ruiz** (Mary) €30 Ⓒ 947 451 125 c/ Pozas N-120. ▮ **Rabé de las Calzadas:** •*Hs* **Fuente de Rabé** *x5* €40-€50 Ⓒ 947 451 191 *www.hostalfuentederabe.com.* ❶ **Libéranos Dómine** *Priv.[24÷4]* €10 Ⓒ 695 116 901 + *menú* €8 + ☛ *La Peña.* ❷ **Óspital Santa Marina y Santiago** *Priv. [8÷1]* €8. •*H* **Camino de Rabé** *x13* €70+ Ⓒ 601 617 639 c/ Alta (+ 300m).

● **Hornillos del Camino:** *AAlb.* ❶ **El Alfar** *Priv.[20÷3]* €12 Ⓒ 619 235 930 + *menú* € 8. ❷ **Meeting Point** *Priv.[32÷3]* €12 *+5* €40+ Ⓒ 608 113 599 *www.hornillosmeetingpoint.com.* ❸ **Hornillos** *Muni.[30÷3]* €10 Ⓒ 689 784 681. ☛ *Casa Manolo* Ⓒ 947 411 050 *menú.* •*CR* **de Sol a Sol** *x7* €40-50 Ⓒ 649 876 091. •*CR* **La Casa del Abuelo** *x5* €45+ Ⓒ 661 869 618.

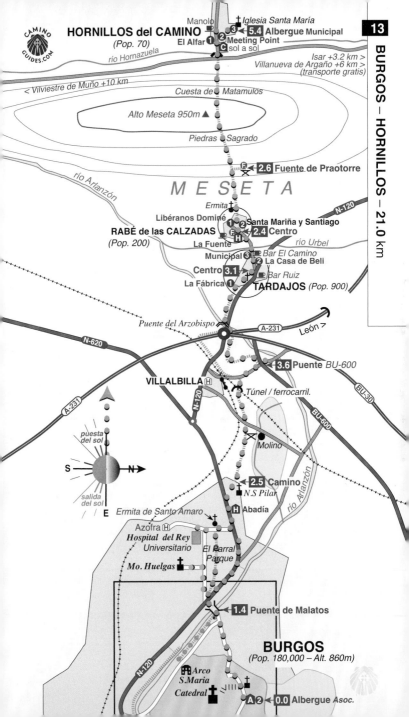

HORNILLOS del CAMINO
(Pop. 70)

Manolo
El Alfar ❶
† Iglesia Santa María
2 Meeting Point ❸ **5.4** Albergue Municipal
C sol a sol

rio Hornazuela

Isar +3.2 km >
Villanueva de Argaño +6 km >
(transporte gratis)

< *Vilviestre de Muño +10 km*

Cuesta de Matamulos

Alto Meseta 950m ▲

Piedras Sagrado

rio Arlanzón

2.6 Fuente de Praotorre

M E S E T A

N-120

Ermita †
Libéranos Domine
❶ **2** Santa Mariña y Santiago
RABÉ de las CALZADAS
(Pop. 200)
2.4 Centro
La Fuente
Municipal ❸ **2** Bar El Camino
rio Urbel
2 La Casa de Beli
Centro **3.1** ❶
† **Bar Ruiz**
La Fábrica ❶
TARDAJOS (Pop. 900)

Puente del Arzobispo
A-231
León >

3.6 Puente BU-600

VILLALBILLA Ⓗ
BU-30
Túnel / ferrocarril.

BU-600

✕ *Molino*

2.5 Camino
■ *N.S Pilar*

Ⓗ Abadía
rio Arlanzón

Ermita de Santo Amaro †
Azofra Ⓗ
Hospital del Rey
Universitario
El Parral
Parque
Mo. Huelgas

1.4 Puente de Malatos

BURGOS
(Pop. 180,000 – Alt. 860m)

🏛 *Arco*
S.María
Catedral †
Ⓐ **2** **0.0** Albergue *Asoc.*

puesta del sol
S ━━⊙━━ N ➤
salida del sol
E

N-620
A-231
N-120
N-120

14 HORNILLOS del CAMINO – CASTROJERIZ

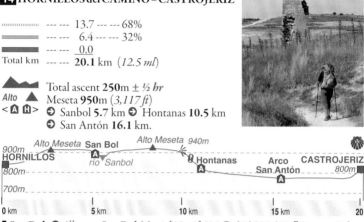

⁞⁞⁞⁞⁞⁞	--- --- 13.7 --- ---	68%
▬▬▬	--- --- 6.4 --- ---	32%
▬▬▬	--- --- 0.0	
Total km	--- --- **20.1** km (*12.5 ml*)	

Total ascent **250**m ± ½ *hr*
Alto ▲ Meseta **950**m (*3,117 ft*)
< **A** **H** > ➲ Sanbol **5.7** km ➲ Hontanas **10.5** km
➲ San Antón **16.1** km.

■ **San Bol:** ●*Albergue* San Bol *Muni.[10÷1]* €10 ☏ 606 893 407. ■ **Fuente Sidres** ●*Alb* Fuente Sidres *Priv.[12÷2]* €15-20 ☏ 686 908 486 www.alberguefuentesidres. es ● **Hontanas:** ❶ Juan de Yepes *Priv.[34÷5]* €12 +4 €55 ☏ 638 938 546 c/ Real 1. ❷ El Puntido *Priv.*[40÷7] €9 +8 €36 ☏ 947 378 597. ❸ Santa Brígida *Priv.*[16÷3] €12 ☏ 628 927 317. ❹ San Juan *Antiguo Muni.[42÷3]* €10-15 ☏ 653 532 647. •*H¨¨*Villa Fontanas *x5* €55 ☏ 680 296 238. •*Hs˙*Fuente Estrella *x6* €35-45 ☏ 646 612 530 •*CR* El Descanso *x8* €55+ ☏ 646 612 530. ■ **San Antón:** ●*Alb.* San Antón *Priv.[12÷1]* €-donativo.

● **CASTROJERIZ:** ❶ *Iglesia Santa María N.S Manzano XIV y museo.* ❷*Iglesia de Santo Domingo y museo.* ❸ *Iglesia San Juan y museo.* ❶ Rinconada *Priv.[18÷1]* €14 +4 €45 ☏ 698 942 323 www.rinconada.net •*Hs˙* El Manzano *x5* €35-46 ☏ 620 782 768. ❷ Orión *Priv.[22÷3]* €13+3 €45+ menú *V.* garden ☏ 649 481 609 c/ Colegiata 28. ❸ Camino de Santiago *Priv.[30÷1]* €6 ☏ 947 377 255 + El Camping €30. **c/Real Oriente:** •*Hs¨* La Cachava ☏ 947 378 547 Nº83. *Alb* ❹ Ultreia *Priv.[28÷2]* €12 +3 €50 ☏ 947 378 640, Nº77, patio and communal dinner. **[+100**m <left]. ❺ A Cien Leguas *Priv.[24÷2]* €12 +6 €40-60 ☏ 947 562 305, Nº72. •*CR* El Veredero €30+ ☏ 696 985 323, Nº78. ❻ Casa Nostra *Priv.[26÷3]* €7 ☏ 947 377 493, Nº54. •*HR* Quinta San Francisco¨¨¨¨ *x21* €120+ ☏ 947 520 262. •*Hs* La Taberna ☏ 947 377 120. ❼ San Esteban *Muni. [35÷1]* €8 ☏ 947 377 001 plaza Mayor. •*Posada* Emebed €45+ ☏ 616 802 473. •*H¨*Iacobus *x14* €39-59 ☏ 947 378 647. ❽ Rosalía *Priv.[30÷3]* €13 +1 €35 ☏ 947 373 714 (Javier) www.alberguerosalia.com

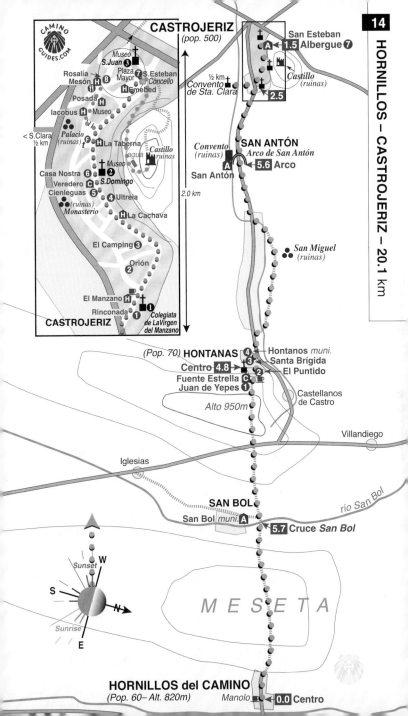

15 CASTROJERIZ – FRÓMISTA
(Burgos)   (Palencia)

-------	--- ---	22.0 --- --- 88%
▬▬▬	--- ---	2.9 --- --- 12%
	--- ---	0.0
Total km	--- ---	**24.9** km (*15.5 ml*)

Total ascent **270**m ± ½ hr
Alto ▲ Alto Mostelares **900**m (*2,952 ft*)
< **A H** > ➲Puente de Itero (S.Nicolas) **8.9**km
➲*Itero del Castillo* **8.9** (*+1.5 km*) ➲Itero de la Vega **10.6** km ➲Boadilla **19.1** km.

● *Itero del Castillo* (*+1.5 km*). *Alb. Mun.[12÷1]* €10 incl. *Menú* © 642 213 560.
▌ **San Nicolás:** *Alb.* San Nicolás *Asoc.[12÷1]* €-donativo. ▌ **Itero de la Vega:** *Hs/
Alb.*❶ **Puente Fitero** *Priv.[22÷2]* €8 +8 €30-40 © 979 151 822 c/ Santa María
(entrada). ❷ **La Mochila** *Priv.[28÷3]* €6-10 *menú* © 979 151 781 c/Santa Ana.
❸ **Hogar del Peregrino** *Priv.[8÷4]* €12 + *menú* © 970 151 86 c/Santa Maria.
❹*Muni.[13÷1]* €5 © 605 034 347 adj. *iglesia San Pedro XVI* Plaza Iglesia.

▌ **Boadilla del Camino:** *Alb.*❶ **En El Camino** *Priv.**[70÷4] €9 © 979 810 284
m:619 105 168 + •*H*̇ Rural en el Camino €35. ❷ **Juntos** *Priv.[12÷1]*+ €12 +
menu €10 *www.juntos-albergue.com*

● **FRÓMISTA** (pop. 800) *Albergues:*
❶ **Frómista** *Muni.[56÷6]* €12 © 979 811
089 / Carmel ©686 579 702 (Carmen)
Plaza San Martín. ❷ **Vicus** *[6÷2]* €10
© 617 483 264 Av. Ingeniero Rivera, 25.
❸ **Luz de Frómista** *[26÷4]* €12 +*1* €34©
979 810 757 Av. del Ejército Español, 10.
❹ **Estrella del Camino** *Priv.[32÷3]* €12
© 979 810 399. ❺ **Betania** *Priv.[9÷2]* ©
638 846 043 €-donativo (winter/invierno)

Hoteles: •*HR*̇ San Martín *x19* €40-60 © 979 810 000. *Av. del Ejército Español
(c/Mayor):* •*Hs*̇ San Pedro *x14* €40+ © 979 810 409. •*Hs*̇ El Apostol *x7* €30+
© 979 810 255. •*Hs*̇ Camino de Santiago *x10* €60 © 979 810 282 •*H*̈ Doña
Mayor *x12* €85+ © 979 810 588 *www.hoteldonamayor.com*. •*H*̈Oasibeth *x14*
€70+ © 979 183 458. •*P* La Vía Láctea *x4* €32+ © 696 009 803 c/ Julio Senador.

○ *Monumentos históricos:* ❶ *Iglesia de San Martín XI.* ❷ *Iglesia de San Pedro
XV.* ❸ *Iglesia Santa María del Castillo* (*Leyenda del Camino*).

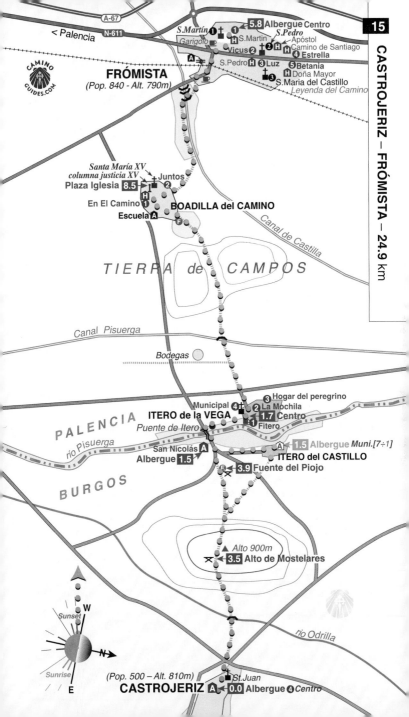

< Palencia

A-67
N-611

FRÓMISTA
(Pop. 840 - Alt. 790m)

CAMINO
GUIDES.COM

S.Martín
Garigolo
5.8 Albergue Centro
H S.Martin
1 Vicus **2**
S.Pedro
Apóstol
2 H Camino de Santiago
S.Pedro **3** Luz
4 Estrella
5 Betania
H Doña Mayor
S.Maria del Castillo
3
Leyenda del Camino

Santa María XV
columna justicia XV
Plaza Iglesia **8.5**
+ Juntos
2
H
1 En El Camino
Escuela **A**
BOADILLA del CAMINO
F

Canal de Castilla

T I E R R A d e C A M P O S

Canal Pisuerga

Bodegas

3 Hogar del peregrino
Municipal **4** **2** La Mochila
ITERO de la VEGA **1.7** Centro
1 Fitero
Puente de Itero
A **1.5** Albergue Muni.*[7÷1]*
San Nicolás **A**
Albergue **1.5**
ITERO del CASTILLO
3.9 Fuente del Piojo

PALENCIA
río Pisuerga

BURGOS

▲ Alto 900m
3.5 Alto de Mostelares

N
W
Sunset

Sunrise
E

río Odrilla

(Pop. 500 – Alt. 810m)
+ St.Juan
CASTROJERIZ **A** **0.0** Albergue **4** Centro

16 FRÓMISTA – CARRIÓN DE LOS CONDES

⸳⸳⸳⸳⸳⸳⸳⸳⸳⸳⸳⸳	--- --- 16.1 --- --- 83%
▬▬▬▬▬	--- --- 3.2 --- --- 17%
▬▬	--- --- 0.0
Total km	--- --- **19.3** km (*12.0 ml*)

Total ascent **50**m ± *0 hr*
Alto ▲ Carrión **830**m (*2,725 ft*)
< 🅰 🏠 > ➲Población **3.4** km ➲Villarmentero **9.3**
➲Villalcázar de Sirga **13.6** km.

■ **Población de Campos:** ●*Alb.* Escuela *Muni.[18÷1]* €5 adj. •*Hs˙*Amanecer *x14* ✆ 979 811 099 €35-50 + *menú* €9. ■ **Villarmentero de Campos:** ●*Alb.* Amanecer *Priv.[18÷2]* €7 + tipi €3! ✆ 629 178 543 *menú* €8. •*CR* Casona de Doña Petra €40 ✆ 979 065 978. ■ **Villalcázar de Sirga** ●*Alb.*Villalcázar *Muni. [20÷2]* €-*donativo* ✆ 979 888 041 Plaza del Peregrino. ●*Alb* Tasca Don Camino *Priv.[26÷3]* €12 ✆ 979 888 163 + •*CR* Don Camino *x7* with menú. •*HsR˙* Infanta Doña Leonor *x11* €45 ✆ 927 888 015 Plaza Mayor. •*CR* Las Cántigas *x5* €30-40 ✆ 979 888 027.

● **CARRION DE LOS CONDES:** ❶ *Turismo* ✆ 979 880 932. ◀*Albergues:* ➊ Santa Clara *Conv.* *[30÷4]* €10 +*9* €25-45 ✆ 979 880 837 *Madres Clarisas.* ➋ Santa María ♥ *Par.[50÷3]* €7 ✆ 979 880 768. ➌ Espíritu Santo *Conv. [90÷7]* €10 Hijas de San Vicente de Paul ✆ 979 880 052 Plaza San Juan. ➍ Casa de espíritualidad N.S de Belén *Conv.[74÷74!]* €25-50 ✆ 979 880 031 *R.R Filipenses.* ◀*Hostales:* •*Hs˙* La Corte *x14* €45 ✆ 979 880 138 c/Santa María, 34. •*Hs*Comfort Suites *x13* €50+ ✆ 639 855 555 c/Santa María, 12 + •*P*El Camino *x2* €30+ ✆ 690 159 596. •*HsR˙* Santiago *x16* €37+ ✆979 881 052 Plaza de los Regentes. •*Hs* Plaza Mayor *x13* €35-50 ✆ 669 340 131 c/Adolfo Suárez, 1. •*Hs* Albe *x8* €30 ✆ 699 094 185 Esteban Colantes,2. •*H¨¨*Real Monasterio San Zoilo *x52* €64-84 ✆ 979 880 050.
Monumentos: ❶ *Museo y Real Monasterio y Ermita de La Piedad XIII.* ❷ *Iglesia de Santa María del Camino XII.* ❸ *Iglesia de Santiago XII museo €1.*

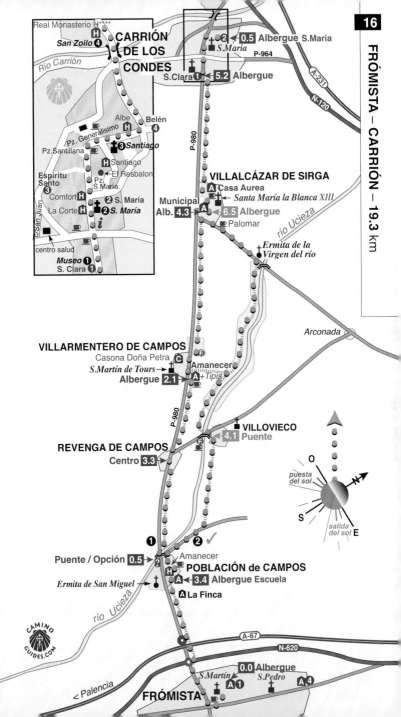

Real Monasterio H****
San Zoilo **4**
CARRIÓN
DE LOS
CONDES

Río Carrión

2 **0.5** Albergue S.Maria
S.Maria
P-964

A-231

N-120

S.Clara **1** **5.2** Albergue

P-980

Albe
Pz. Generalísimo
Belén **4**
Pz.Santillana
3 Santiago
Santiago
El Resbalon
Espiritu Santo **3**
Pz. S.María
Comfort
S. María **2** S. María
La Corte
i

centro salud

Museo **1**
S. Clara **1**

C/San Juan

VILLALCÁZAR DE SIRGA
Casa Aurea
Santa María la Blanca *XIII*
Municipal
Alb. **4.3**
6.5 Albergue
Palomar

rio Ucieza

Ermita de la
Virgen del río

Arconada

VILLARMENTERO DE CAMPOS
Casona Doña Petra
S.Martín de Tours →
Amanecer
Albergue **2.1**
Tipis

P-980

VILLOVIECO
4.1 Puente

REVENGA DE CAMPOS
Centro **3.3**

1
2 ✓

Puente / Opción **0.5** →
Amanecer
POBLACIÓN de CAMPOS
Ermita de San Miguel
3.4 Albergue Escuela
La Finca

río Ucieza

A-67

N-620

S.Martín **0.0** Albergue
S.Pedro
1
4
FRÓMISTA

< Palencia

O
puesta del sol
S
salida del sol E

CAMINO GUIDES.COM

17 CARRIÓN de los CONDES – TERRADILLOS de los TEMPLARIOS

--- --- 18.7 --- --- 70%
--- --- 8.1 --- --- 30%
--- --- 0.0
Total km **26.8** km (*16.7 ml*)

Total ascent **100**m ± *¼ hr*
Alto Ledigos alto **900**m (*2,950 ft*)
<A H> Calzadilla de la Cueza **17.3** km
Ledigos **23.4** km.

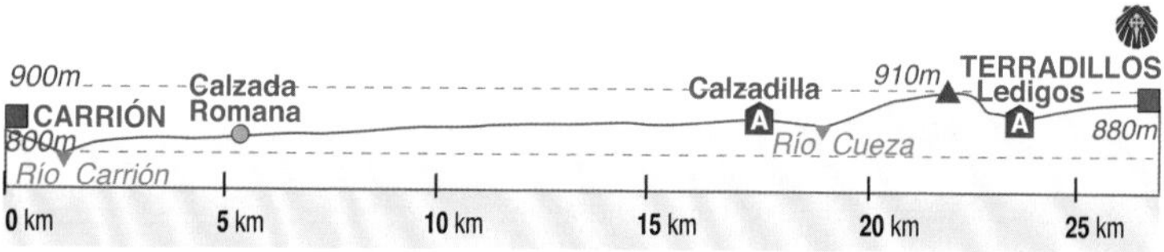
900m
CARRIÓN
800m
Río Carrión
Calzada
Romana
Calzadilla
Río Cueza
910m
Ledigos
TERRADILLOS
880m
0 km
5 km
10 km
15 km
20 km
25 km

▌Calzadilla de la Cueza: ❶ Calzadilla *Muni.*[34÷2]* €8 © 670 558 954. ❷ Camino Real *Priv.*[80÷2]* €12 © 979 883 187 *menú* €10. ❸ Los Canarios *Priv.*[11÷3]* €15-19 © 659 976 894. •*Hs* Hostal Camino Real *x18* €50 © 979 883 187. **▌Ledigos:** ❶ El Palomar *Priv.*[47÷2]* €8 +*5* €20 © 979 883 605 c/ Ronda de Abajo. ❷ La Morena *Priv.[18÷1]* €15 +*10* €40-55 © 979 065 052 *www.alberguelamorena.com* c/ Carretera 3.

● **Terradillos de los Templarios:** ❶ Los Templarios *Priv.[52÷6]* €12 +*9* €28-38 © 979 065 968 *menú*. ❷ Jacques de Molay *Priv.*[50÷8]* €12 © 979 883 679 *menú* c/ Iglesia, 18.

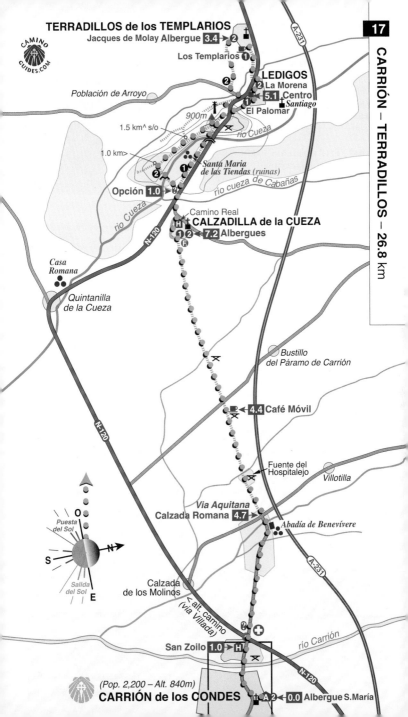

TERRADILLOS de los TEMPLARIOS

Jacques de Molay Albergue **3.4** ❷

Los Templarios ❶

❷

LEDIGOS

❷ La Morena

❶ **5.1** ⬛ Centro

⬛ *Santiago*

El Palomar

Población de Arroyo

900m

1.5 km^ s/o

1.0 km>

❷

❶ *Santa Maria de las Tiendas (ruinas)*

rio Cueza

rio cueza de Cabañas

Opción 1.0 ▶

Camino Real

Ⓗ **CALZADILLA de la CUEZA**

❶❷ **7.2** Albergues

Ⓕ

rio Cueza

Casa Romana

Quintanilla de la Cueza

Bustillo del Páramo de Carrión

⬛ **4.4** Café Móvil

Fuente del Hospitalejo

Villotilla

Via Aquitana
Calzada Romana **4.7** ▶

Abadía de Benevívere

O
Puesta del Sol

S

Salida del Sol E

N-120

Calzada de los Molinos

< alt. camino (via Villada)

San Zoilo **1.0** ▶ Ⓗ

rio Carrión

N-120

(Pop. 2,200 – Alt. 840m)
CARRIÓN de los CONDES

⬛Ⓐ❷ **0.0** Albergue S.María

CAMINO GUIDES.COM

18 TERRADILLOS de los Templarios – ❶ BERCIANOS del Real Camino
(via SAHAGÚN) ❷ CALZADILLA de los Hermanillos

....	--- ---	19.6 --- --- 83%
▭▭▭	--- ---	3.7 --- --- 16%
▬▬▬	--- ---	0.2 --- --- 01%
Total km		**23.5** km (*14.6 ml*)

Total ascent **0**m ± *0 hr*
Alto ▲ Terradillos **880**m (*2,890 ft*)
< 🅰 🄷 > ❺Moratinos **3.2** km ❺ San Nicolás **6.0**
❺ Sahagún **13.0** ❺ Calzada del Coto **18.3** km

TERRADILLOS *880m*
900m Moratinos San Nicolás SAHAGÚN *Calzada de Coto* BERCIANOS
800m *Río Sequillo* *Río Cea* CALZADILLA
00 km 5 km 10 km 15 km 20 km 25 km

■ **Moratinos:** *Alb.*❶ Moratinos *Priv.[16÷4]* €10 +5 €50 ✆ 979 061 466 c/ Real.
❷ **San Bruno** *Asoc.[30÷1]* €9 +2 €40 ✆ 979 061 465 c/ Ontanón. •*CR* El Castillo
x4 ✆ 979 061 467 ■ **San Nicolás del Real Camino** (*Palencia*): ●*Alb.* Laganares
Priv.*[*20÷4*] €10 +*1* €30 ✆ 979 188 142, Pl. Mayor.

● **SAHAGÚN** (*León*): **p.54**

❶ *Real Camino* ● ● ● Bercianos *del Real Camino*: ❶ La Perala *[56÷1]*
€12 ✆ 685 817 699 c/ Camino Santaigo Frances. ☞ *Casa Peregrino* adj. *Alb*
❷ Bercianos1900 *Priv.[20÷2]* €15 Marta Sanahuja ✆ 987 784 244 c/ Mayor
2 terraza & ⊪/🍴. •*Hs* Rivero *x8* €45 ✆ 987 744 287 + ⊪/🍴. ❸ Santa Clara
Priv.[10÷2]+ €10 +*6* €40 Rosa Fures ✆ 987 784 314. *Alb.* ❹ Bercianos Casa
Rectoral ♥ *Par.[44÷5]* €-donativo ✆ 987 784 008. •*CR* El Sueve *x4* €45 ✆ 987
784 139 + ⊪/🍴

❷ *Via Romana* ● ● ● Calzada del Coto ●*Alb.*San Roque *Muni.[15÷2]*
€-donativo ✆ 987 781 233 c/Real. ■ Calzadilla de los Hermanillos: *Alb.* ❶
Via Trajana *Priv.[10÷3]* €15 +5 €50 ✆ 987 337 610 *www.alberguevíatrajana.
com* c/Mayor + *menú*. ❷ Calzadilla *Muni.[24÷6]* €-donativo ✆ 987 330 013.
•*HR* Casa El Cura *x7* €65 ✆ 987 337 647 c/La Carratera 13.

Real Camino ❶
Francesa

Via Romana ❷
Trajana

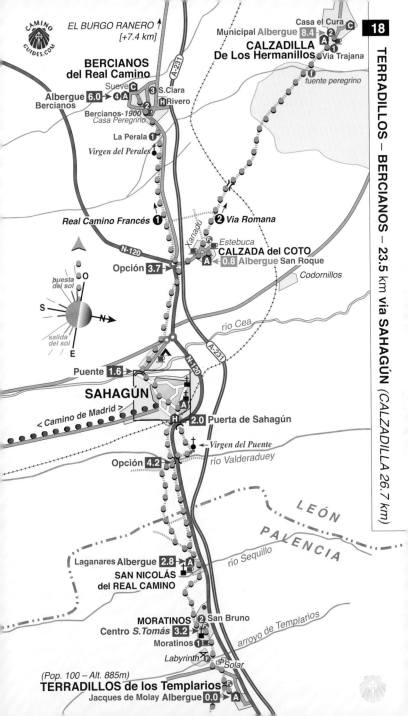

EL BURGO RANERO ↑
[+7.4 km]

Casa el Cura **C**
Municipal **Albergue** 8.4 → **A** 2
CALZADILLA
De Los Hermanillos Via Trajana
fuente peregrino

BERCIANOS
del Real Camino

Sueve **C**
Albergue 6.0 → 4 **A**
Bercianos
3 S.Clara
2 **H** Rivero
Bercianos-1900
Casa Peregrino

La Perala 1
Virgen del Perales

Real Camino Francés 1

2 *Via Romana*

Yanadú
Estebuca
CALZADA del COTO
A ← 0.8 **Albergue San Roque**

N-120
Opción 3.7
Codornillos

río Cea

A-231

Puente 1.6
N-120

SAHAGÚN
A

< Camino de Madrid >
H 2.0 **Puerta de Sahagún**

† ← *Virgen del Puente*
Opción 4.2
río Valderaduey

LEÓN
PALENCIA

río Sequillo

Laganares Albergue 2.8 → **A**
SAN NICOLÁS
del REAL CAMINO

MORATINOS 2 San Bruno
Centro *S.Tomás* 3.2
Moratinos 1
Labyrinth **F**
Solar

(Pop. 100 – Alt. 885m)
TERRADILLOS de los Templarios
Jacques de Molay Albergue 0.0 → **A**

arroyo de Templarios

puesta del sol
O
S ● N
salida del sol
E

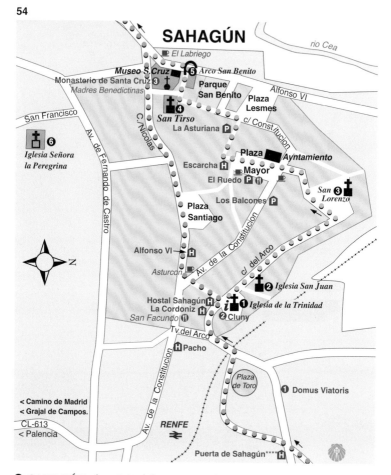

54

SAHAGÚN

● **SAHAGÚN:** *(pop. 2,800)* ❶ *Turismo:* Iglesia Trinidad c/ del Arco ✆ 987 782 117 ○**Monumentos:** ❶ *Iglesia de la Trinidad XIII–XVII (municipal albergue + Turismo)*❷ *Iglesia San Juan XVII (San Facundo y Primitivo).* ❸ *Iglesia San Lorenzo XII (Mudejar).* ❹ *Iglesia San Tirso (Mudejar ruinas)* Parque San Benito. ❺ *Arco San Benito* y *Monasterio y Museo de Santa Cruz museo (Madres Benedictinas).* ❻ *Iglesia Señora La Peregrina XV.*

❰*Albergues:* ❶ **Domus Viatoris** *Priv.*[50÷6]* €7+*12* €25 ✆ 987 780 975 Travesía del Arco. ❷ **Cluny** *Muni.[64÷1]* €5 ✆ 987 782 117 *(iglesia de la Trinidad y Turismo).* ❸ **Monasterio de Santa Cruz** *(Madres Benedictinas) Conv.[58÷9]* €6 +*10* €20. ✆ 650 696 023 c/ Nicolas 40. ❰*Hoteles:* •*Hs*˙˙˙**Puerto de Sahagún** €25 •*Hs*˙˙**La Cordoniz** *x20* €40-50 ✆ 987 780 276 c/ del Arco opp. Turismo. •*Hs*˙ **La Bastide Du Chemin** *x9* €45 ✆ 987 781 183 c/ del Arco, 66. •*Hs*˙˙**Alfonso VI** *x14* €35 ✆ 987 781 144 c/Nicolás, 4. •*Hs* **Don Pacho** ✆ 987 780 775 Av. Constitución, 84. •*Hs*˙ **El Ruedo II** *x5* €50 ✆ 987 781 834 Plaza Mayor, 1. •*Hs*˙˙ **Escarcha** *x14* €22-40 ✆ 987 781 856 c/Regina Franco, 12. •*P* **Los Balcones del Camino** €30 ✆ 676 838 242 c/ Juan Guaza 2 (Av. Constitución 53).

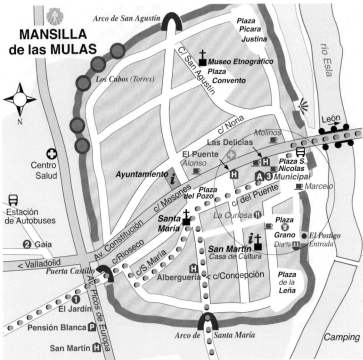

● **MANSILLA DE LAS MULAS:** *(pop: 1,900)* ⊙ *Turismo* ℂ 987 310 012 Plaza del Pozo. **Convento de San Agustín** *Museo Etnográfico* c/ Agustín (10:00-14:00 / 16:00-19:00).

◖*Albergues: Alb.*❶ **El Jardín del Camino** *Priv.[40÷2]* €12 ℂ 987 310 232 *www.albergueeljardindelcamino.com* c/Camino de Santiago 1. ❷ **Gaia** *Priv.[16÷2]* €10 ℂ 987 310 308 m: 699 911 311 (Marisa) Av. Constitución 28. *Alb.* ❸ **Centro Muni.[74÷8]** €5 ℂ 987 311 250 c/del Puente 5 - *cerrado temporalmente 2023.* ◖*Hostales (centro):* ⑪•*Hs˙* **El Puente** *x12* €35-€66 ℂ 987 310 762 c/Mesones Nº12 and at Nº20-22 ⑪•*Hs* **Las Delicias** *x9* €25-€40 ℂ 987 310 558. •*Hs˙˙˙* **Alberguería del Camino** *x4* €38-€56 ℂ 987 311 193 c/Concepción 12. •*P˙* **Blanca** *x7* €25-40 ℂ 626 003 177 Av. Picos de Europa 4. •*HR* **La Casa de los Soportales** *x10* €30-50 ℂ 987 310 232, Pl. Arrabal, 9. •*Hs˙* **San Martín** *x10* €30-45 ℂ 987 310 094.

19 BERCIANOS — MANSILLA
del Real Camino   de las Mulas

ⅢⅢⅢⅢⅢⅢ	--- --- 23.1--- ---	87%
▬▬▬▬	--- --- 3.6--- ---	13%
▬▬▬	--- --- 0.0 --- ---	0%
Total km	**26.7** km (*16.7 ml*)	

Total ascent **0**m ± *0 hr*

Alto ▲ El Burgo Ranero **880**m (*1,669 ft*)
< Ⓐ Ⓗ > ↻ El Burgo Ranero **7.4** km
        ↻ Reliegos **20.5** km.

BERCIANOS 850m
900m ■Calzadilla   El Burgo Ranero
                                    Ⓐ   Reliegos
800m   río Fuentes   río Valdecasa   Ⓐ   MANSILLA
                                      río Valdearcos
00 km   5 km   10 km   15 km   20 km   25 km

❶ *Real Camino* ●●●Ⅰ**El Burgo Ranero:** ●*Alb.* Domenico Laffi *Asoc.[30÷4]*
€-*donativo* ℂ 987 330 023 c/Fray Pedro. ●*Alb.* **La Laguna** *Priv.[20÷2]* €12 +5
€40 ℂ 987 330 094 c/La Laguna *(Piedras Blancas).* •*Hs* **el Peregrino** *x10* €30-45
ℂ 987 330 069 •*H* **Piedras Blancas** *x10* €40 ℂ 987 330 094. •*P* **La Costa del
Adobe** *x4* €40 ℂ 676 550 508. 🍴 *El Camino (Paella!)* ℂ 674 58 39 47 c/ Real 53.
(+500 m Aviva ⅼ•*H* **Castillo El Burgo** *x25* €60 ℂ 987 330 403 Ⅰ **Villarmarco** ●
+1 km ●*Alb.* **La Vieja Escuela** *Priv.[8÷3]* €5 ℂ 657 958 092.

● **Reliegos:** •*P* **La Cantina de Teddy** *x4* €50+ ℂ 987 190 627. ***Calle Real Nº56***
❶ **Vive tu Camino** *Priv.[20÷2]* €10 +*1* €45 ℂ 987 317 837. @*Nº42* ❷ **Las
Hadas** *Priv.[20÷3]* €12 +*2* €40 ℂ 691 153 010 *www.alberguelashadas.com.*
Centro 🍴*Gil* 🍴 *Elvis /* 🍴 *La Torre (Sinín)* [⛺] adj. ❸ **Gil** *Priv.[14÷2]* €13 + €30
ℂ 987 317 804 & 🍴 + 400m ❹ **D.Gaiferos** *Muni.[44÷4]* €5 ℂ 987 317 801 c/
Escuela adj. ❺ **La Parada** *Priv.[36÷6]* €12 +*2* €40 ℂ 987 317 880 + ⅼ/🍴

❷ *Via Romana* ●●● **Reliegos** *opción (+ 1.0 km)*

● **MANSILLA de las MULAS** *p.55*

Reliegos:

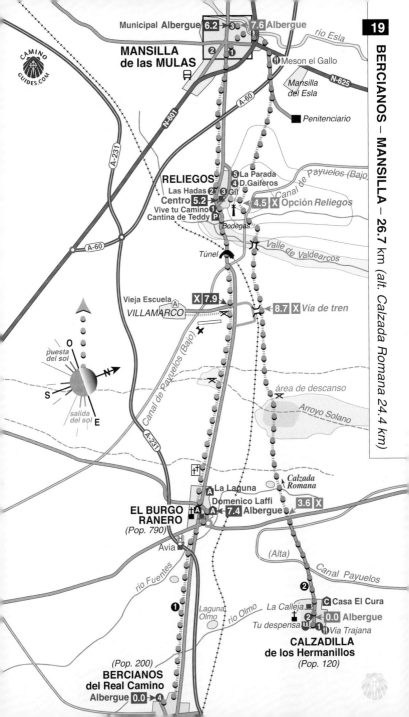

19

BERCIANOS — MANSILLA — 26.7 km (alt. Calzada Romana 24.4 km)

MANSILLA de las MULAS

Municipal **Albergue** **6.2** ➔ 3. **7.6** **Albergue**

2 **1**

1 Meson el Gallo

Mansilla del Esla

N-625

A-60

■ *Penitenciario*

Canal de Payuelos (Bajo)

5 La Parada
4 D. Gaiferos
RELIEGOS
Las Hadas **2** **3** Gil
Centro **5.2** ✕
Vive tu Camino **1** **P**
Cantina de Teddy

4.5 ✕ **Opción** *Reliegos*

Bodegas

Valle de Valdearcos

Túnel

A-60

Vieja Escuela **✕** **7.9**
A
VILLAMARCO

8.7 ✕ *Vía de tren*

Canal de Payuelos (Bajo)

A-231

O
puesta del sol
N
S
E
salida del sol

área de descanso

Arroyo Solano

Calzada Romana

A La Laguna
Domenico Laffi **A** **A** **7.4** **Albergue**

3.6 ✕

EL BURGO RANERO
(Pop. 790)
A **A**
H
Avia

río Fuentes

(Alta)

Canal Payuelos

2

1

Laguna Olmo
río Olmo

La Calleja
Tu despensa

C Casa El Cura
2 **0.0** **Albergue**
1 **1** *Via Trajana*

CALZADILLA de los Hermanillos
(Pop. 120)

(Pop. 200)
BERCIANOS del Real Camino
Albergue **0.0** ➔ 4

río Esla

CAMINO GUIDES.COM

20 MANSILLA de las MULAS – LEÓN

....	--- ---	10.2 --- ---	56%
	--- ---	3.5 --- ---	20%
	--- ---	4.4 --- ---	24%
Total km		**18.1** km	(*11.2 ml*)

Total ascent **160**m ± ¼ *hr*

Alto ▲ Alto del Portillo **890**m (*2,920 ft*)

< A H > ➲ Villarente **6.1** km ➲ Arcahueja **10.6** km ➲ Puente Castro **15.6** km.

900m
MANSILLA ■800m
Vilarente
río Porma
Arcahueja
Valdelafuente
Alto del Portillo
Puente Castro
829m
LEÓN
río Torio
00 km — 5 km — 10 km — 15 km

❚ **Puente Villarente:** *Alb.*❶ **El Delfín Verde** *Priv.[20÷3]* €5 *+15* €30–€45 *©* 987 312 065 *www.complejoeldelfinverde.es*. ❷ **San Pelayo** *Priv.**[57÷4]* €8 *+10* €33-43 *©* 987 312 677 *www.alberguesanpelayo.com*. •*Hs* **La Montaña** *x14* €40 *©* 987 312 161. ☞ *Hs* **Avellaneda** *x2* €25-40 *©* 987 312 040. ❚ **Arcahueja:** ●*Alb.* **La Torre** *Priv.[22÷2]* €10 *+4* €30 *©* 987 205 896. ❚ **Valdelafuente:** •*Hs**** **Camino Real** *x44* €40 *©* 987 218 134 (*+300m*). ❚ **Puente Castro:** ●*Alb.* **Santo Tomás de Canterbury** *Priv.[48÷3]* €10 *+3* €50 *©* 987 392 626 + ¶▮☞ Av. de La Lastra (*Citroën*). ●*Alb.* **Check in León** *Priv.[40÷2]* €11 *©*987 498 793 Alcalde Miguel Castaño 88.

● **LEÓN** *p.60*

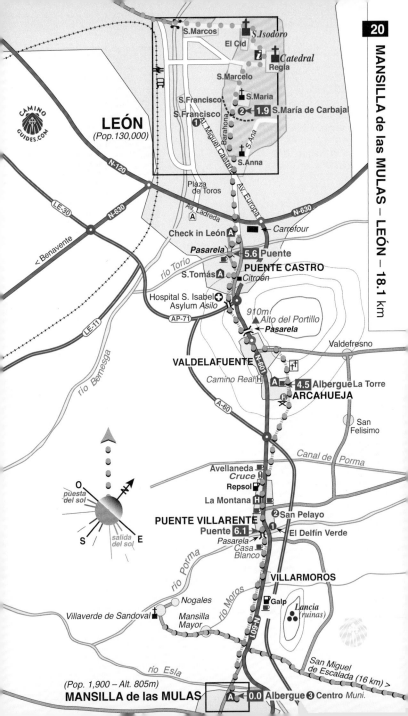

LEÓN
(Pop.130,000)

CAMINO
GUIDES.COM

S.Marcos
El Cid
S.Isodoro
Catedral
Regla
i
S.Marcelo
S.Francisco
S.Francisco
S.Maria
S.María de Carbajal
Barahona
S.Ana
S.Anna
2 **1.9**

N-120
N-630
LE-30
N-630
< Benavente
N-630

Plaza
de Toros
Av. Ladreda
Av. Europa
Carrefour
Check in León
Pasarela
5.6 Puente
PUENTE CASTRO
rio Torio
S.Tomás
Citroën
Hospital S. Isabel
Asylum *Asilo*
AP-71
LE-11
rio Bernesga
910m
Alto del Portillo
Pasarela
Valdefresno
VALDELAFUENTE
Camino Real
4.5 AlbergueLa Torre
ARCAHUEJA
A-60
San
Felisimo
Canal de Porma
Avellaneda
Cruce
Repsol
La Montana
PUENTE VILLARENTE
Puente **6.1**
San Pelayo
2
1 El Delfín Verde
Pasarela
Casa
Blanco
rio Porma
VILLARMOROS
Galp
Lancia
(ruinas)
Nogales
Villaverde de Sandoval
Mansilla
Mayor
rio Moros
LE-60

O
*puesta
del sol*
S
E
*salida
del sol*

rio Esla
(Pop. 1,900 – Alt. 805m)
MANSILLA de las MULAS
San Miguel
de Escalada (16 km) >
A **0.0** Albergue **3** Centro *Muni.*

LEÓN *(pop: 130,000)* **Centro:** ❶ *Turismo:* Plaza Regla (Catedral) Ⓒ 987 237 082 ❖*Credencial Asociación de Amigos del Camino* Av. Independencia, 5º Ⓒ 987 260 530 / 677 430 200. *Equipos peregrino y guias:* Armería Castro c/La Rúa 7 Ⓒ 987 257 020.

○ *Monumentos históricos:* ❶ *Puerta Moneda* *(muralla romana)* ❷ *Iglesia de S. María del camino* (Mercado) *XII.* ❸ *Iglesia S.Marcelo XII - XVII.* ❹ *Casa Botines (Gaudí).* ❺ *Palacio Guzmanes XVI (+ patio).* ❻ *Catedral Pulchra Leonina XIII (museo + claustro).* ❼ *Basilica de San Isidoro XII (Misa del peregrino 19:30).* ❽ *Panteón Real XI.* ❾ *San Marcos (Museo / Parador / Claustro XII– XVI).*

◀*Albergues:* ❶ San Francisco de Asís *Residencia Fundación Ademar Asoc.* *[70÷23]* €12-18 +*11* €50 Ⓒ 987 215 060 Av. Alcalde Miguel Castaños, 4 (adj. *Jardin San Franciso).* ❷ S.María de Carbajal *Conv.[134÷4]* €8 Ⓒ 680 649 289 Plaza Grano / Santa María del Camino. ❸ Alda *Priv.[40]* €14 Ⓒ 987 192 035 www.aldahotels.es Pl. Don Gutierre, 1. ❹ Muralla Leonesa *Priv.[60÷12]* €15 +*8* €40 Ⓒ 987 177 873, c/ Tarifa, 5. ❺ LeónHostel €21 per persona + €45 Ⓒ 987 079 907 c/ Ancha 8. ❻ Unamuno *Priv.[86÷28]* €13-18 Ⓒ 987 233 010 www.albergueunamuno.com c/ San Pelayo, 15. ❼ *Hs* Zentric *Priv.[8÷2]* €21 per persona + €50 Ⓒ 636 946 294 c/ Legión VII, 6/ 2º.

◀*Hoteles* €30-€60: •*P* Sandoval *x8* Ⓒ 987 212 041 c/Hospicio, 11-2º. •*H*˙˙˙ Monástica Pax *x20* €70+ Ⓒ 987 344 493 Plaza Grano, 11 (adj. alb.1). •*H*˙ Rincón del Conde Ⓒ 987 849 021 Conde Rebolledo. •*Hr*˙˙˙La Posada Regia I & II Ⓒ 987 213 173 c/Regidores, 9. •*H*˙˙˙ París Ⓒ 987 238 600 c/Ancha, 18. •*HsR*˙Albany *x13* Ⓒ 987 264 600 La Paloma,13. •*H*˙˙˙ Le Petit Leon *x16* Ⓒ 987 075 508 c/ Del Pozo, 2. •*H*˙˙˙NH Plaza Mayor *x51* €80+ Ⓒ 987 344 357 Plaza Mayor,15. ◀*Cathedral*: •*H*˙˙ QH Ⓒ 987 875 580 Av.Los Cubos,6. •*Hs*˙Fernando I Ⓒ 987 220 601 Av.Los Cubos,32. •*Hs*˙˙Alda Casco Antiguo *x12* Ⓒ 987 074 000 c/Cardenal Landázuri,11. ◀*Otros*: •*HsR*˙ Guzmán el Bueno *x25* Ⓒ 987 236 412 c/López Castrillón, 6. •*HsR*˙San Martín Ⓒ 987 875 187 Plaza Torres de Omaña, 1. •*HsR*˙˙Boccalino Ⓒ 987 220 017 Plaza S. Isodoro, 1. •*HsR*˙˙˙San Idodoro Ⓒ 987 875 088 Plaza Santo Martino. •*Hr*˙Reina Ⓒ 987 205 212 c/Puerta de la Reina, 2. •*HsR*˙Alvarez Ⓒ 987 072 520 c/Burgo Nuevo, 3. •*H*˙˙˙Alfonso V Sercotel Ⓒ 987-220 900 Av. Padre Isla, 1. •*HsR*˙ Padre Isla II Ⓒ 987 228 097 Av.Padre Isla, 8 / •*HsR*˙ Padre Isla Ⓒ 987 092 298 Joaquín Costa,2. ◀*Estación de tren:* •*H*˙˙ Orejas Ⓒ 987 252 909 c/Villafranca, 8. •*P*˙ Blanca Ⓒ 987 2521 991 c/Villafranca, 2. •*HsR*˙˙ Don Suero Ⓒ 987 230 600 Av. Suero de Quiñones, 15. •*H*˙˙˙˙Parador San Marcos Ⓒ 987 237 300 €100+. •*Hs*˙˙Quevedo *x20* Ⓒ 987 242 975 Av. Quevedo

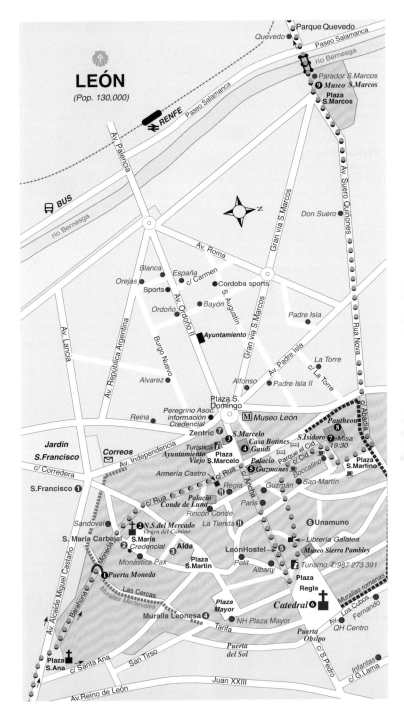

21 LEÓN – ❶ VILLADANGOS del PÁRAMO
❷ *VILLAR DE MAZARIFE*

⋯⋯⋯	--- --- 9.8 --- ---	46%
▬▬▬	--- --- 5.4 --- ---	25%
▬▬	--- --- 6.1 --- ---	29%
Total km	**21.3** km (*13.2 ml*)	

Total ascent **250**m ± ½ *hr*
Alto ▲ Páramo **901**m (*2,956 ft*)
< 🅐 🅗 > ➲Virgen del Camino **8.5** km ➲Valverde
➲Oncina – **9.8** km.

[elevation profile: 900m, LEÓN, río Bernesga 800m, Alto Cruceiro, La Virgen, Valverde, S.Miguel, río Oncina, Chozas de Abajo, MAZARIFE, VILLADANGOS — 00 Km, 5 km, 10 km, 15 km, 20 km]

▌**Trobajo del Camino:** •*Hs* **Abuelo** *x26* €55 ℂ 987 801 044 c/Mesones.

● **LA VIRGEN DEL CAMINO N-120** •*H*··· **VillaPaloma** *x44* €40-60 ℂ 987 300 990.•*Hs* **Julio Cesar** *x8* €20-40 ℂ 987 302 044 c/Cervantes. •*Hs* **San Froilán** *x22* €30-€50 ℂ 987 302 019 / •*Hs*·· **Plaza** *x9* €30-€50 on c/Peregrino. •*Hs*** **Soto** *x28* €30-50 ℂ 987 802 925, N-120. •*Hs* **Central** *x25* €25 ℂ 987 302 041. ●*Alb.* **D.Antonio y Dña.Cinia** *Muni.*[*40÷2*] €7 ℂ 987 302 800 c/Camino de Villacedré (*adj. Seminario on Av. Padre Eustoquio*).

❶ ● ● ● *Via Villadangos:* ▌**Valverde de la Virgen:** ●*Alb.* **La Casa del Camino** *Priv.*[*22÷1*] €15 ℂ987 303 455 c/ El Jano. ● **Villadangos del Páramo:** •*Hr*·· **Avenida III** *x65* €60 ℂ 987 390 311. ●*Alb.* **Villadangos** *Asoc.*[*50÷7*] €7 ℂ 671 010 786. •*Hs* **Alto Páramo** *x16* €60 ℂ 987 390 347. ▲**Camping Camino de Santiago** ℂ 987 680 253 (+300m).

❷ ● ● ● *Via Mazarife:* ▌**Oncina** ●*Alb.* **El Pajar** *Priv.*[*9÷1*] €10 incl. +€35 menú €9 ℂ 677 567 309 c/Arriba 4. •*H* **Domus Oncinae** *x15* €50 *www.domusoncinae.com* c/Real, 7 ● **Mazarife:** *Alb.* ❶ **San Antonio de Pádua** *Priv.* [*50÷3*] €10 +5 €50 *cena comunitaria* ℂ 987 390 192. ❷ **Casa de Jesús** *Priv.* [*50÷10*] €9 ℂ 987 390 697. ❸ **Tio Pepe** *Priv.*[*22÷5*] €12 (€22 media pensión) +*6* €50 ℂ 987 390 517 + 📱

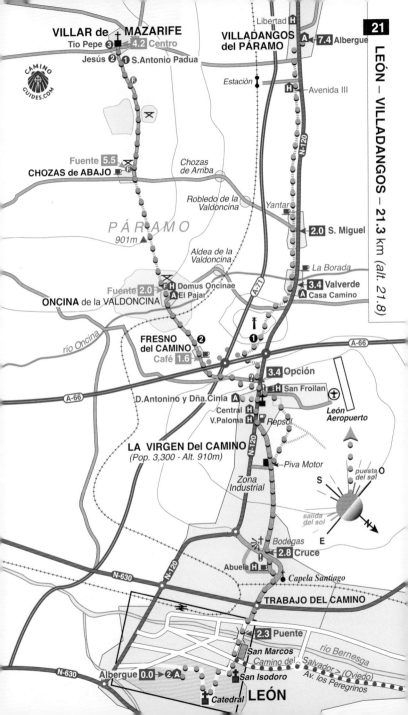

Libertad **H**

VILLADANGOS del PÁRAMO

A ◄ **7.4** Albergue

VILLAR de MAZARIFE
Tio Pepe **3** **4.2** Centro

Jesús **2** **1** S.Antonio Padua

Estación

H — Avenida III

Fuente **5.5**

CHOZAS de ABAJO

Chozas de Arriba

Robledo de la Valdoncina

Yantar

2.0 S. Miguel

P Á R A M O

901m ▲

Aldea de la Valdoncina

La Borada

3.4 Valverde

A Casa Camino

Fuente **2.0** **H** Domus Oncinae

A El Pajar

ONCINA de la VALDONCINA

río Oncina

FRESNO del CAMINO **2**

Café **1.6**

3.4 Opción

A-66

A-71

A-66

León Aeropuerto

D. Antonino y Dña. Cinia **A**

H San Froilan

Central **H**

V.Paloma **H**

Repsol

LA VIRGEN Del CAMINO
(Pop. 3,300 - Alt. 910m)

Piva Motor

puesta del sol

O

S

E

salida del sol

Zona Industrial

Bodegas

2.8 Cruce

Abuela **H**

Capela Santiago

TRABAJO DEL CAMINO

río Bernesga

2.3 Puente

San Marcos
Camino del

Salvador > (Oviedo)

Av. los Peregrinos

Albergue **0.0** ► **2 A**

San Isodoro

Catedral **LEÓN**

N-630

N-120

N-120

N-630

22 ❶ VILLADANGOS – ASTORGA
❷ *MAZARIFE – PUENTE DE ÓRBIGO*

┈┈┈┈┈┈	--- --- 22.2 --- ---	78%
▬▬▬▬	--- --- 5.8 --- ---	20%
▬▬▬▬	--- --- 0.5 --- ---	02%
Total km	**28.5** km (*17.7 ml*)	

Total ascent 250m ± ½ hr
Alto ▲ Santo Toribio **905**m (*2,970 ft*)
< Ⓐ Ⓗ > ⟿San Martín **4.7** km
⟿Hospital de Órbigo **11.3** km ⟿Villares **14.4** km ⟿Santibáñez **16.9** km
⟿San Justo **24.9** km. (❷ *Alt. route* Mazarife via the Páramo ⟿Villavante **9.9** km)
❶ ● ● ● *Via Villadangos:* ▮**San Martín del Camino:** N-120: Alb.❶ Vieira

Elevation profile:
MAZARIFE — S.Martín — Villavante — HOSPITAL DEL ÓRBIGO — Santibañez — Alto S.Toribio 925m — ASTORGA
VILLADANGOS 800m — Canal — río Órbigo — S.Justo río Tuerto
0 km — 5 km — 10 km — 15 km — 20 km — 25 km — 30

Priv.[36÷6] €10 +2 Ⓒ 987 378 565 d *V. comida vegetariana.* ❷ La Huella *Priv.[30÷3]* €12 +10 €45 Ⓒ 640 846 063 *www.alberguelahuella.com.* ❸ Santa Ana *Priv.[40÷2]* €7 +12 €25-35 Ⓒ 654 111 509. ❹ La Casa Verde *Priv.[10÷1]* €10 Ⓒ 646 879 437 (Beatriz Puente) Travesía de La Estación 8. ❺ San Martín *Muni.[46÷2]* €6 Ⓒ 676 020 388. ▮**Puente de Órbigo:** •B&B Puente de Órbigo *x3* €50 Ⓒ 630 149 922.

❷ ● ● ● *Via Mazarife:* ▮**Villavante:** •*Alb.* Santa Lucía *Priv.[22÷1]* €10 +3 €45 Ⓒ 987 389 105. •*CR* Molino Galochas *x5* €55 Ⓒ 987 388 546.

● **HOSPITAL DE ÓRBIGO:** ❶ La Encina *Priv.[16÷4]* €11 +3 €40 Ⓒ 987 361 087 Av. de Suero de Quinoñes. ▲camping *municipal.* •*Hs¨*Don Suero de Quiñones *x11* €50-70 Ⓒ 987 388 238. ❷ Karl Leisner *Par.[92÷10]* €5 Ⓒ 987 388 444. ❸Casa de los Hidalgos *[18÷1]* €12 +3 €35+ Ⓒ 699 198 755 ❹ San Miguel *Asoc.*[30÷4] €10 Ⓒ 987 388 285 *www.alberguesanmiguel.com.* ❺ Verde *V. Priv.[26÷2]* €11 Ⓒ 689 927 926 *www.albergueverde.es.* Av. Fueros de León •*Hs¨*Cantón Plaza *x5* €50 Ⓒ 987 388 896 c/Santos Olivera, 27. c/Sierra Pambley: @Nº40 •*CR¨* N.S. de Lourdes *x9* €40 Ⓒ 987 388 253. Nº56 •*CR* El Caminero *x5* €40 Ⓒ 987 389 020. •*H¨*El Paso Honroso *x37* €60 Ⓒ 987 361 010, N-120.

▮**Villares de Órbigo:** *Alb.*❶ El Encanto *Priv.[10÷1]* €14 +6 €40-50 *albergueelencanto.es* ❷ Villares *Priv.[19÷4]* €12 +3 €40 Ⓒ 947 132 935 *www.alberguevillaresdeorbigo.com* ▮**Santibáñez de Valdeiglesia:** *Alb.* ❶ Santibáñez *Par.[20÷4]* €8 Ⓒ 987 377 698. ⚑ *Centro Social.* c/ Real: ❷ Camino Francés *Priv.[24÷2]* €10 Ⓒ 987 361 014. ❸ L'Abilleiru *x6* €27 por persona +3 €50 Ⓒ 615 269 057 *www.labilleirualberguerural.com* menú €9. ▮**San Justo de la Vega:** •*Hs¨* Juli *x12* €25-45 Ⓒ 987 617 632.

● **ASTORGA** p.66

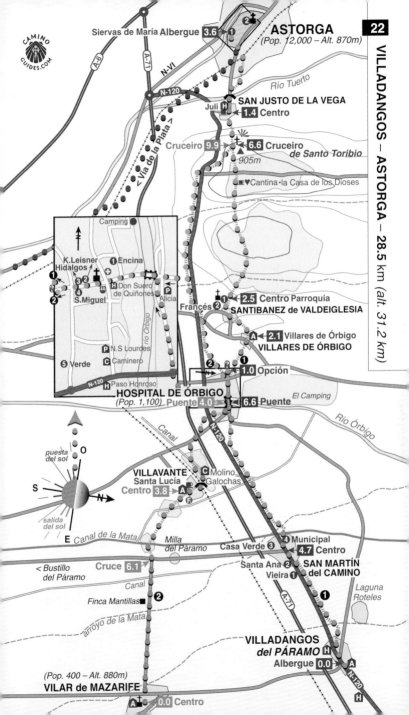

Siervas de María Albergue **3.6** ❶

ASTORGA
(Pop. 12,000 – Alt. 870m)
❷ ✝

Río Tuerto

SAN JUSTO DE LA VEGA
Juli Ⓗ
◀ **1.4** Centro

Cruceiro **9.9** ✝ **6.6** Cruceiro *de Santo Toribio*
905m

▥♥Cantina·la Casa de los Dioses

Camping ●

K.Leisner ❶ Encina
Hidalgos Ⓗ
❶ ③❷ ✝ Ⓗ Don Suero
④ de Quiñones
❷ S.Miguel Ⓟ
Alicia
Francés ✝ ❷ **2.5** Centro Parroquia
SANTIBANEZ de VALDEIGLESIA

Ⓟ N.S Lourdes Ⓐ **2.1** Villares de Órbigo
Ⓒ Caminero **VILLARES DE ÓRBIGO**
❺ Verde

❷ ❶ **1.0** Opción
Ⓗ Paso Honroso
HOSPITAL DE ÓRBIGO ↯ **6.6** Puente
(Pop. 1,100) Puente **4.0** El Camping

Río Órbigo

Canal *N-120*

puesta
del sol O

VILLAVANTE Ⓒ Molino
Santa Lucía Galochas
Centro **3.8** Ⓐ
Ⓕ

*salida
del sol*

E Canal de la Mata

Milla
del Páramo Casa Verde ❸ ❹ Municipal
◀ **4.7** Centro
< Bustillo Cruce **6.1** Santa Ana ❷ **SAN MARTÍN**
del Páramo Vieira ❶ **del Camino**

Canal

Finca Mantillas ■ ❷ ❶ *Laguna
Roteles*

A-71

VILLADANGOS
del PÁRAMO Ⓗ
Albergue **0.0** Ⓐ
N-120
Ⓗ

(Pop. 400 – Alt. 880m)
VILAR de MAZARIFE
Ⓐ ✝ **0.0** Centro

ASTORGA: *(pop: 12,000)* ❶ *Turismo:* © 987 618 222 Glorieta Eduardo Castro. ○ *Monumentos:* ❶ *Plaza San Francisco Convento de San Francisco / Murallas Romano (ruinas).* ❷ *Plaza Bartolomé Iglesia San Bartolomé / Ergástula (museo).* ❸ *Plaza Mayor (Plaza España) Ayuntamiento.* ❹ *Plaza Santocildes Museo del Chocolate.* ❺ *Plaza Obispo Alcolea Puerta de Rey / Casa Granell.* ❻ *Plaza Catedral Palacio Episcopal* (Gaudí) *Museo de los Caminos* y *Cruz de Ferro / Iglesia de Santa Marta / Catedral XV Museo de Catedral.*

◖*Albergues:* *Alb.*MyWay *Priv.[13÷1]* €12 +5 €40-60 © 640 176 338 c/San Marcos, 7. *Central:* *Alb.*❶ Siervas de María *Asoc.[156÷20]* €7 © 987 616 034 Plaza San Francisco. ❷ Só Por Hoje *Priv.[10÷1]* €25 incl. +€65 © 690 749 853 *www.alberguesoporhoje.com* c/Rodríguez de Cela, 30. ❸ San Javier *Asoc.**[110÷5] €10 © 987 618 532 c/Portería, 6.

◖*Hostales: (*€40-60*):* •*H¨* La Peseta *x15* © 987 617 275 + ⅋ *Maragatería* Plaza San Bartolomé, adj. •*H¨¨* Spa Vía De La Plata c/Padres Redentoristas, 5 © 987 619 000 •*H¨¨* Astur Plaza *x37* © 987 617 665 on Plaza Mayor (España). •*H¨* Imprenta Musical *x24* © 987 045 704 c/ del Arzobispo López Peláez, 6 (adj. Casa Sacerdotal). •*H¨¨* Casa de Tepa *x9* © 987 603 299 c/Santiago,2. •*H¨¨* Ciudad De Astorga Spa *x33* © 987 603 001 c/ los Sitios,7. •*H* El Descanso de Wendy *x6* © 987 617 854 c/ Matadero Viejo, 11. •*H¨¨* Gaudí *x35* © 987 615 654 opp. Gaudí palace. ◖*Otros:* •*Hs¨* Coruña *x17* © 987 615 009 Av. de Ponferrada, 72. ⅋/•*Hs* Delfín *x12* © 987 602 414 + 1.1 km.

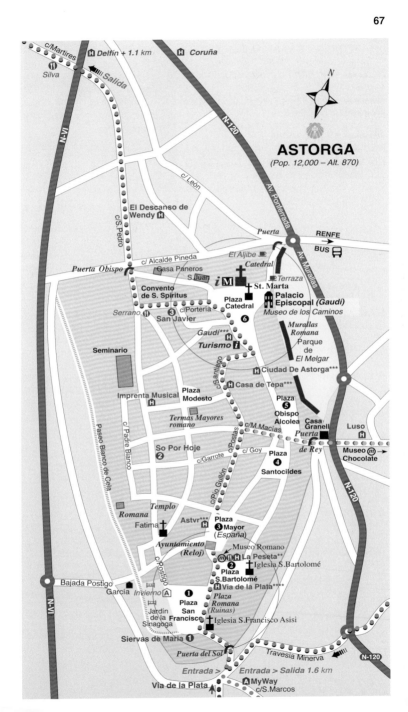

ASTORGA
(Pop. 12,000 – Alt. 870)

c/Martires
H *Delfin* + 1.1 km   **H** *Coruña*

H *Silva*

Salida

N-120

N-VI

Puerta   **RENFE**

BUS

c/León

H El Descanso de Wendy

c/S.Pedro

c/ Alcalde Pineda

El Aljibe

Catedral

Terraza

Puerta Obispo

Casa Paneros

S.Juan

i **M**   † **St. Marta**

Palacio Episcopal *(Gaudi)*

Convento de S. Spiritus

Plaza Catedral

Museo de los Caminos

Serrano **H**

3

San Javier

c/Portería

6

Gaudí***

Murallas Romana

Parque de El Melgar

H *Turismo* **i**

c/Santiago

H **Ciudad De Astorga*****

Seminario

H Casa de Tepa***

Plaza **5** Obispo Alcolea

Casa Granell

Luso

H Imprenta Musical

Plaza Modesto

c/M.Macias

Puerta

Museo *m* **→ Chocolate**

c/ Padre Blanco

Termas Mayores romano

c/Crosta

de Rey

H

So Por Hoje **2**

c/Garrote

c/ Goy

Plaza **4** Santocildes

Paseo Blanco de Cela

c/Pio Gullón

Templo Romana

Fatima †

Astvr***

Plaza **3** Mayor *(España)*

Ayuntamiento *(Reloj)*

Museo Romano

m **H** La Peseta**

H † Iglesia S.Bartolomé

Plaza **2** S.Bartolomé

c/Postigo

Bajada Postigo

H Via de la Plata****

García *Invierno* **A**

Plaza Romana (Ruinas)

N-VI

Jardín de la Sinagoga

Plaza San **1** Francisco

† Iglesia S.Francisco Asisi

Siervas de Maria 1

Puerta del Sol

Travesia Minerva

N-120

Entrada >

Entrada > Salida 1.6 km

A MyWay c/S.Marcos

Via de la Plata

23 ASTORGA – RABANAL del CAMINO

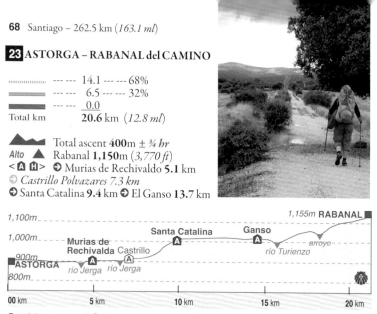

```
............  --- ---  14.1 --- --- 68%
━━━━━━━  --- ---   6.5 --- --- 32%
━━━━━  --- ---   0.0
Total km        20.6 km  (12.8 ml)
```

Total ascent **400**m ± ¾ *hr*
Alto ▲ Rabanal **1,150**m (*3,770 ft*)
< Ⓐ Ⓗ > ➲ Murias de Rechivaldo **5.1** km
➲ *Castrillo Polvazares 7.3 km*
➲ Santa Catalina **9.4** km ➲ El Ganso **13.7** km

[Elevation profile]
1,100m — 1,155m **RABANAL** ■
Santa Catalina — Ganso
1,000m — Murias de — arroyo
Rechivalda — Castrillo — Ⓐ — rio Turienzo
900m — Ⓐ — Ⓐ — rio Jerga — Ⓐ
■ASTORGA — rio Jerga — rio Jerga
800m —
00 km — 5 km — 10 km — 15 km — 20 km

■ **Valdeviejas:** *Alb.●* **Ecce Homo** *Muni.[10÷4]* €5 © 620 960 060. ■ **Murias de Rechivaldo:** *Alb.* ❶ **Casa las Águedas** *Priv.[30÷2]* €15 +5 €55+ © 987 691 234. ❷ **Escuela** *Muni.[10÷1]* €9 © 638 433 716. ❸ **Casa Flor** *[20÷4]* €15 +8 €55 © 644 695 872. •*CR* **La Valeta** x5 €55 © 616 598 133.

● **Castrillo de Polvazares** ●*Alb.* de Peregrinos *Muni.[8÷1]* €5 © 691 221 058 c/ del Jardín •*Cr* **Flores Del Camino** x2 €50-60 © 691 221 058 c/ Real 36. •*Hs* **Cuca La Vaina** x7 €60 © 9987 691 034 c/del Jardin. ¶/•*CR* **Casa Coscolo** x4 €50 © 987 691 984 c/La Magdalena.

■ **Santa Catalina:** *Alb.*❶ **El Caminante** *Priv.[22÷2]* €10 +12 €30-45 ©987 691 098. ❷ **Hospedería San Blas** *Priv.[20÷2]* €10 +8 €30-40 © 987 691 411. ❸ **La Bohéme** *[10÷2]* €-donativo © 658 262 257 •*H* **Via Avis** x6 €75 ©987 199 319 c/ El Sol, 21 ■ **El Ganso** ●*Alb.* **Indian Way** *Priv.[27÷3]* €10 © 691 545 004 c/ Los Peregrinos [+200m]. ●*Alb.* **Gabino** *Priv.[24÷3]* €10 © 625 318 585.

● **RABANAL DEL CAMINO:** *c/ Real:* ¶/•*Hs* **La Candela** x6 €50 © 987 691 810. *Alb.* ❶ **La Senda** *Priv.[24÷4]* €10 © 696 819 060 adj. •*P* **El Tesín** x4 €50 © 635 527 522 🛏 *V./* ▲ opp. **Green Garden** 🛏/🍴/▲ *(Hevia).* •*CR* **The Stone Boat** x3 €40+ © 652 660 504. ✝*Iglesia Santa María* XII[b]*c.* ❷ **Gaucelmo** *Asoc.* *[36÷3]* €-donativo © 987 631 751. ❸ **N.S del Pilar** *Priv.[76÷2]* €10 +4 €35 © 987 631 621. ❹ *Muni.[36÷2]* €10 © 987 631 687. ●**Benedictine Monastery** *San Salvador del Monte Irago* €-donativo © 987 631 528 *www. monteirago.org/en/.* •*P* **La Casona** x6 €37-45 © 625 470 392 pl./Jerónimo Morán, 15. •*H* **Casa Indie** x5 €50 © **Alba** 625 470 392 c/ Medio 4a. •*Hs* **El Refugio** x16 €50 © 987 631 592 ¶/🛏. •*H¨*La Posada de Gaspar* x14 €55 © 987 631 629.

```
```

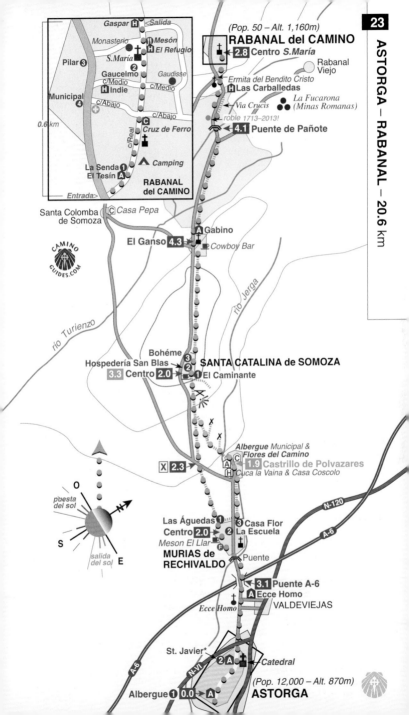

(Pop. 50 – Alt. 1,160m)
RABANAL del Camino

2.8 Centro *S.María*

Rabanal Viejo

Ermita del Bendito Cristo
Las Carballedas

La Fucarona
(Minas Romanas)

Vía Crucis

roble 1713–2013!

4.1 Puente de Pañote

Inset map:

Gaspar H ·Salida·

Monasterio
Mesón
H El Refugio

S.María

Pilar 3

Gaucelmo
H Indie

Gaudisse

Municipal 4

c/Abajo

0.6 km

C
Cruz de Ferro

c/Real

Camping

La Senda 1
El Tesín A

·Entrada·

RABANAL del Camino

Santa Colomba de Somoza — C *Casa Pepa*

A Gabino

El Ganso 4.3

Cowboy Bar

río Jerga

río Turienzo

Bohéme
3
Hospedería San Blas 2
3.3 Centro 2.0 1 El Caminante

SANTA CATALINA de SOMOZA

Albergue Municipal &
Flores del Camino

A
C 1.9 Castrillo de Polvazares
H *Cuca la Vaina & Casa Coscolo*

X 2.3

O

puesta del sol

S

salida del sol

E

Las Águedas 1
3 Casa Flor
Centro 2.0 2 La Escuela
Meson El Llar F

MURIAS de RECHIVALDO

Puente

3.1 Puente A-6
A Ecce Homo

Ecce Homo

VALDEVIEJAS

N-120

A-6

St. Javier*
2 A
Catedral

(Pop. 12,000 – Alt. 870m)

Albergue 1 0.0 A
ASTORGA

24 RABANAL del CAMINO – MOLINASECA

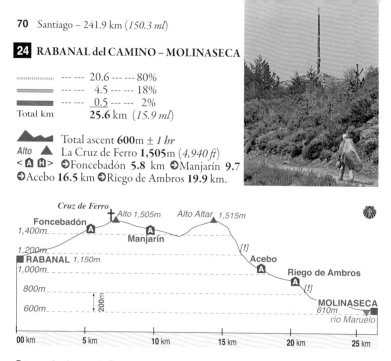

┈┈┈	─── ─── 20.6 ─── ───	80%
━━━	─── ─── 4.5 ─── ───	18%
━━━	─── ─── <u>0.5</u> ─── ───	2%
Total km	**25.6 km** (*15.9 ml*)	

Total ascent **600m** ± *1 hr*
Alto ▲ La Cruz de Ferro **1,505**m (*4,940 ft*)
< Ⓐ Ⓗ > ➲Foncebadón **5.8** km ➲Manjarín **9.7**
➲Acebo **16.5** km ➲Riego de Ambros **19.9** km.

■ **Foncebadón:** *Alb.* ❶ Roger de Lauria *(Convento de Foncebadón) Priv.[24÷4]*
€12 +*14* €35-50 © 987 053 934 (Jessica & Marcos) ☙/menú. ❷ Casa Chelo *Priv.*
[8÷1] €15-20 © 641 023 636 ❸ Monte Irago *Priv.[35÷2]* €10 incl. © 695 452
950. ❹ La Posada del Druida *Priv.[20÷3]* €12 +*6* €50 © 987 053 928. ❺ La
Cruz de Ferro *Priv.[34÷2]* €15 © 669 752 144. ❻ Domus Dei *Par.[18÷1]*
€-d*onativo.* •*P* El Trasgu *x4* €39+ © 987 053 877.

■ **Manjarín** ●*Alb.* Manjarín *Priv.[35÷1]* €5. ■ **Acebo:** ❶ Mesón El Acebo *Priv.*
[32÷2] €7 +*2* €24 © 987 695 074 ❷ Apóstol Santiago *Par.[22÷1]* €-*donativo*
❸ La Casa del Peregrino *[80÷10]* €12 +*7* €45-60 © 987 057 793. *Hostales:*
(€40-60): •*CR* La Rosa del Agua *x3* © 616 849 738. •*CR* La Casa del Peregrino
x5 © 987 057 875. •*CR* La Trucha del Arco Iris *x3* © 987 695 548. ■ **Riego de
Ambros:** ●*Alb.* Riego de Ambros *Muni.[26÷2]* €8 © 987 695 190.

● **MOLINASECA (€35-55):** •*HsR¨* El Palacio *x15* © 987 453 094 adj. •*Hs*
The Way *x5* © 637 941 017 c/El Palacio. •*Hs* El Horno *x5* © 987 453 203 c/
El Rañadero 3 •*CR* San Nicolas *x6* © 630 111 846 c/ La iglesia Nº43 & @ Nº3
●*Alb.* Compostela *Priv.[32÷2]* €10 © 987 453 057. c/Real ●*Alb.* Señor Oso
Priv.[16÷3] €12 © 661 761 970. •*H* Molina Real *x9* €50+ © 987 453 123. •*CR*
Torre de Babel © 987 453 064. •*CR* El Reloj *x8* © 987 453 124. •*CR* Pajarapinta
x8 © 987 453 040 •Casa Morrosco *x9* €25 © 635 807 060. •*H¨* Floriana €55 ©
987 453 146 Av. Fraga Ibibarne. •*H* Capricho de Valérie *x8* €65 © 987 831 683.
•*H* NoMad Green *x22* €50+ © 987 453 146

+**0.5 km** - c/ *Fraga Iribarne: Alb.* ❶ Santa Marina *Priv.*[38÷3]* €10 +*4* €40 ©
987 453 077. ❷ San Roque *Mun.[20÷1]* €10 © 600 501 030.

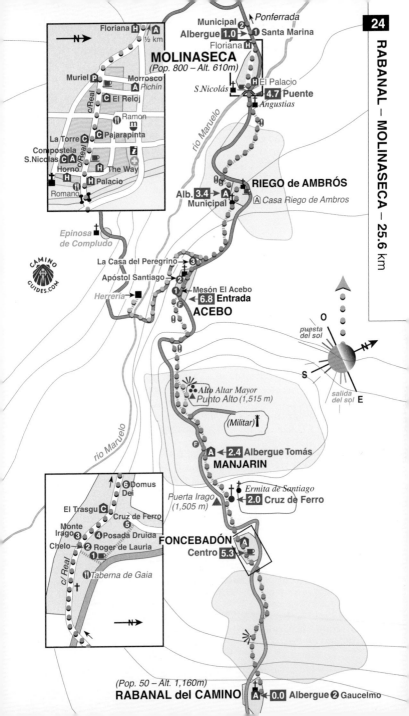

Ponferrada

Municipal
Albergue `1.0` → 1 Santa Marina
Floriana **H**

MOLINASECA
(Pop. 800 – Alt. 610m)

H El Palacio
S.Nicolás
`4.7` **Puente**
Angustias

rio Maruelo

RIEGO de AMBRÓS

Alb. `3.4` → A
Municipal   A *Casa Riego de Ambros*

*Epinosa
de Compludo*

La Casa del Peregrino → 3
Apóstol Santiago → 2
Herrería   1 ← Mesón El Acebo
      F   `6.8` **Entrada**
      ACEBO

**Alto Altar Mayor
Punto Alto** (1,515 m)

(Militar)

F   A `2.4` **Albergue Tomás**
      MANJARÍN

✝ *Ermita de Santiago*
Puerta Irago   `2.0` **Cruz de Ferro**
(1,505 m)

FONCEBADÓN
Centro `5.3`   A

rio Maruelo

(Pop. 50 – Alt. 1,160m)
RABANAL del CAMINO   A `0.0` **Albergue** 2 Gaucelmo

Molinaseca inset

Floriana **H** A
½ km

Muriel **P**   Morrosco
      A *Pichín*
      C El Reloj

      Ramon
      m
La Torre **C**   **C** Pajarapinta
Compostela **C A**
S.Nicolás
Horno **H**   **H** The Way
      H Palacio
Romano

Foncebadón inset

6 Domus
Dei
El Trasgu **C**
      Cruz de Ferro
Monte   5
Irago 3   4 Posada Druida
Chelo   2 Roger de Lauria
      1
      1 Taberna de Gaia

c/ Real

Compass rose

O
puesta
del sol   N
S
salida
del sol   E

25 MOLINASECA – VILLAFRANCA DEL BIERZO
(*via PONFERRADA*)

⬝⬝⬝⬝⬝⬝ --- ---	10.0 --- ---	33%
▬▬▬ --- ---	16.5 --- ---	54%
▭▭▭ --- ---	4.1 --- ---	13%
Total km	**30.6** km (*19.0 ml*)	

Total ascent **200m** ± ¼ **hr**

Alto ▲ Alto Villafranca **550m** (*1,805 ft*)

<🅐 🅗> ➲ Ponferrada **5.3**km ➲ Camponarya **16.6** km➲ Cacabelos **22.0** km
➲ Pieros **24.9** km ➲Valtuille **26.3** km

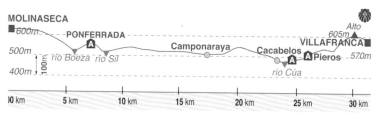

● **PONFERRADA** *p.74* ● **VILLAFRANCA DEL BIERZO** *p.75*

▮**Compostilla:** •*H¨*Novo *x56* €55 ✆ 987 424 441 N-IV. ▮**Columbrianos:** •*CR* Almendro De María *x7* €50+ ✆ 633 481 100 c/ Real 56. ▮**Camponaraya Fuentes Nuevas:** [*El Camino* ✆ 672 057 061 c/ Médicos sin Fronteras, 8 + 500m]. ●*Alb.* Naraya *Priv.[26÷5]* €9 ✆ 987 459 159 Av. de Galicia, 506. ●*Alb.* La Medina *Priv.[18÷1]* €10 + €45 ✆ 987 463 962 Av. Camino de Santiago, 87. •*Hs¨* Camponaraya *x4* ✆ 619 279 931 Av. Camino de Santiago, 50.

● **CACABELOS:** •*H¨* Moncloa de San Lázaro *x8* €85 ✆ 987 546 101 Plaza San Lázaro. *Iglesia Santa María XVI.* ➊**Turismo** ✆ 987 546 011. •*H¨¨* Villa *x30* €36 ✆ 987 548 148. c/*Santa Maria:* •*Hs* Saint James Way €20 por persona ✆ 987 037 871. •*Hs¨* Santa María *x20* €45 ✆ 987 549 588. ●*Alb.* El Molino *Priv.[16÷4]* €15 +*4* €30 ✆ 987 546 829. ●*Alb.* La Gallega *Priv.[29÷7]* €15 +*19* €30-46 ✆ 987 549.

▮ **Las Angustias** ●*Alb.* Cacabelos *Muni.[70÷35]* €6 ✆ 987 547 167 Plaza del Santuario adj. *Capilla de Las Angustia XVIII.*

●●●● +**3** km X*ᵗʰ*c **Monasterio de Santa Maria** (*San Salvador*) **de Carrecedo.** ●Ubaldo Nieto *Priv. x8* €49 ✆ 608 888 211.

▮ **Pieros** ●*Alb.* El Serbal y la Luna *Priv.*[20÷3] €10 *V.* ✆ 639 888 924 / 987 54 60 44. ▮ **Valtuille de Arriba:** ●*Alb.* Acogida La Biznaga *Priv.*[5÷2] €-donativo ✆ 682 187 093 c/ Platería, 33.

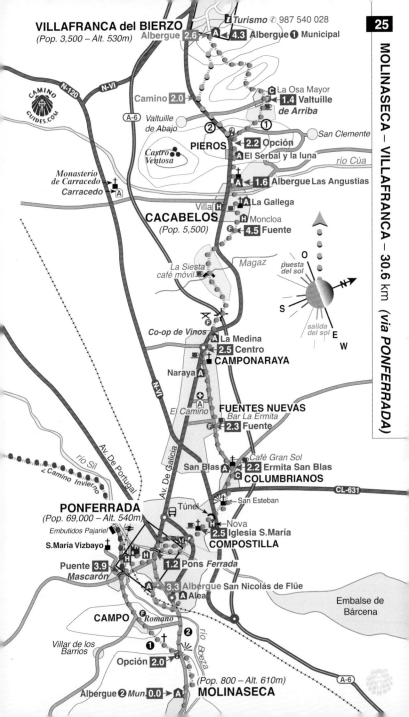

VILLAFRANCA del Bierzo
(Pop. 3,500 – Alt. 530m)

Albergue **2.6** → A **4.3** Albergue ❶ Municipal

i *Turismo* © 987 540 028

CAMINO GUIDES.COM

N-120 N-VI

N-VI

Camino **2.0**

A-6   Valtuille de Abajo

C La Osa Mayor
F **1.4** Valtuille *de Arriba*

② ①

San Clemente

2.2 Opción

PIEROS

A El Serbal y la luna

río Cúa

Castro Ventosa

Monasterio de Carracedo
✝
Carracedo   A

A **1.6** Albergue Las Angustias

A La Gallega

Villa H
CACABELOS
(Pop. 5,500)

H Moncloa
F **4.5** Fuente

Magaz

La Siesta café móvil

puesta del sol

O

N

S   salida del sol   E

W

Co-op de Vinos

A La Medina
2.5 Centro
CAMPONARAYA

Naraya A

A
El Camino
A

FUENTES NUEVAS
Bar La Ermita
F **2.3** Fuente

río Sil

Av. De Portugal

< Camino Invierno

Av. De Galicia

N-VI

Café Gran Sol
✝
San Blas A **2.2** Ermita San Blas
C **COLUMBRIANOS**

CL-631

✝ ← San Esteban

Túnel

H ← Nova

PONFERRADA
(Pop. 69,000 – Alt. 540m)

Embutidos Pajariel

S.María Vizbayo

H **2.5** Iglesia S.María
COMPOSTILLA

M

H H

1.2 Pons *Ferrada*

Puente **3.9**
Mascarón

A **3.3** Albergue San Nicolás de Flüe

A Alea

CAMPO   F *Romano*

❷

Villar de los Barrios

✝   ❶

río Boeza

Opción **2.0**

Embalse de Bárcena

A-6

Albergue ❷ *Mun.* **0.0** → A   **MOLINASECA**
(Pop. 800 – Alt. 610m)

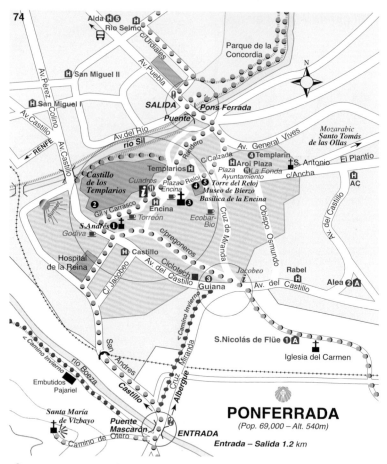

● **PONFERRADA:** *(pop. 69,000)* ❶ *Turismo:* © 987 424 236 c/ Gil y carrasco, 4. *Monumentos:* ❶ *Iglesia San Andrés XVII (Cristo del Castillo).* ❷ *Castillo de los Templarios XII.* ❸ *Basílica de la Encina XVI* Plaza Virgen de la Encina. ❹ *Cárcel Real XVI y Museo del Bierzo.* ❺ *La Torre del Reloj XVI.*

◖*Albergues:* ❶ San Nicolás de Flüe *Par.[186÷7]* €-donativo © 987 413 381 c/de la Loma (Av. del Castillo). ❷ Alea *Priv.[18÷4]* €13 Communal dinner €8 *V.option* © 987 404 133 *www.albergealea.com* c/Teleno, 33. ❸ Guiana *Priv. [90÷14]* €12 +6 €60 © 987 409 327 *www.albergueguiana.com* Av. del Castillo 112. ❹ El Templarín *[24÷2]* €15 © 987 192 619 c/ La Calzada, 4. ❺ Alda *[40÷5]* €16 +46 €50 © 987 790 219 Av. de la Puebla, 44.

◖*Hoteles Centro:* •*Hs¨* Rabel *x10* © 987 417 176 & *Nº115* •*H¨¨* El Castillo *x48* © 987 456 227. •*Hs¨* Virgen de la Encina *x13* © 987 409 632 c/ Comendador. •*Hs¨* Los Templarios *x18* © 987 411 484 c/ Flores Osorio. •*H¨¨* Aroi Bierzo Plaza © 987 409 001 Plaza del Ayuntamiento. *Otros:* •*Hs˙* Río Selmo *x17* © 987 402 665 c/Río Selmo,22. •*H¨¨* Alda Centro *x46* © 987 411 550 •*Hs* San Miguel *x15* © 987 426 700 c/Juan de Lama,14.

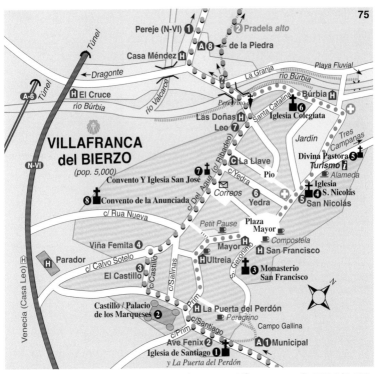

● **VILLAFRANCA DEL BIERZO:** *(pop. 3,500)* ❶ *Turismo* ⓒ 987 540 028 Av. Bernardo Díez Olebar. *Monumentos Históricos:* ❶ *Iglesia de Santiago XI Puerta de Perdón.* ❷ *Castillo Palacio de los Marqueses XV.* ❸ *Monasterio de San Francisco* c/San Geronimo. ❹ *Iglesia San Nicolás XVII.* ❺ *Convento Divina Pastora.* ❻ *Iglesia Colegiata (Iglesia N.S. de Cluniaco).* ❼ *Convento y Iglesia de San José XVIII.* ❽ *Convento de la Anunciada.*

◖*Albergues:* ❶ Municipal *[60÷3]* €7 ⓒ 987 542 356. ❷ Ave Fenix *Asoc.[80÷5]* €10 ⓒ 987 540 229. *menú comunitarias* €7 / *Queimada.* ❸ El Castillo *Priv. [16÷2]* €10 ⓒ 987 540 344 (Marta y Javi) c/ El Castillo 8. ❹ Viña Femita *Priv. [20÷2]* €14 +9 €59 ⓒ 987 542 490 a/Calvo Sotelo, 2. ❺ Hospedería San Nicolás El Real *Priv.[75÷4]* €10 +14 €50 ⓒ 696 978 653 c/Travesía de San Nicolás adj. Plaza Mayor. ❻ La Yedra *[18÷1]* €10 ⓒ 636 586 872 c/ La Yedra, 9. ❼ Leo *Priv. [24÷7]* €12 ⓒ 987 542 658 (María Gallego) c/Ribadeo 10 (c/ del Agua). ❽ de la Piedra ♥ *Priv.*[12÷2]* €12 +4 €30 ⓒ 987 540 260 c/Espíritu Santo,14.

◖*Hoteles:* •*H*```` Parador *x51* €75+ ⓒ 987 540 175 Av. Calvo Sotelo. •La Puerta del Perdón *x7* €50 ⓒ 987-540 614 Plaza Prim,4. *Adj. Plaza Mayor* €40-60: •*Hs* Ultreia *x4* ⓒ 987 540 391 Puentecillo. •*H*```Posada Plaza Mayor *x15* ⓒ 987 540 620. •*H* San Francisco ⓒ 987 540 465. •*CR* La Llave *x2* ⓒ 987 542 739 c/del Agua,37. •*H*`` Las Doñas del Portazgo *x17* €66+ ⓒ 987 542 742. •*Hs*`` Búrbia *x10* ⓒ 987 542 667 Fuente Cubero, 13. •*Hs*`` Tres Campanas *x7* ⓒ 670 359 692 Av. Paradaseca 27 (+500m). *Adj. rio* €30-55: •*Hs*`` Casa Méndez *x12* ⓒ 987 540 055 c/Espíritu Santo 1. •*Hs* Cruce *x13* ⓒ 647 715 755 c/San Salvador 41. •*Hs* Venecia *x4* €12 / €25-40 ⓒ 629 206 074 €12 c/ Peña Picón 5.

26 VILLAFRANCA del BIERZO – O'CEBREIRO

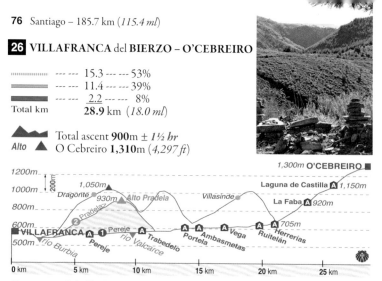

....	--- ---	15.3 --- ---	53%
	--- ---	11.4 --- ---	39%
	--- ---	2.2 --- ---	8%
Total km		**28.9** km (*18.0 ml*)	

Total ascent **900m** ± *1½ hr*
Alto ▲ O Cebreiro **1,310**m (*4,297 ft*)

1,300m O'CEBREIRO ■
1200m
1,050m
1000m
Dragonte · 930m · Alto Pradela · Villasinde · Laguna de Castilla ⒶⒶ 1,150m
800m · La Faba Ⓐ 920m
600m · Pradela · 705m
VILLAFRANCA Ⓐ ❶ · Pereje · Ⓐ Trabadelo · Ⓐ Portela · Ⓐ Ambasmetas · Vega · Ⓐ Herrerías · Ruitelán
500m · río Burbia · Pereje · río Valcarce
0 km   5 km   10 km   15 km   20 km   25 km

➲ **Ruta Pradela** ●*Alb.* **Lamas** *Priv.[10÷1]* €10 ℭ *677 569 764 + 1 km Pradela].*
➲ **Ruta Pereje:** ●*Alb.* **Pereje** *Muni.[30÷2]* €5 ℭ 987 540 138. •*CR* **Las Coronas** *x4* €40. ■ **Trabadelo:** ❶ **Crispeta** *Priv.[32÷5]* €12 ℭ 987 566 529. ❷ **Casa Susi** *[8÷1]* €12 ℭ 683 278 778 menu *V..* ❸ **Parroquial** *[20÷3]* €7 *+1* €20 ℭ 630 628 130. ❹ **Camino y Leyenda** *Priv.[8÷2]* €17 *+4* €35 ℭ 628 921 776. ❺ **Municipal** *[36÷6]* €9 ℭ987 566 447. •*CR* **Os Arroxos** *x8* €25-40. •*CR* **El Puente Peregrino** *x3* €30-38 ℭ987 566 500 *V.* menu. •*Hs* **Nova Ruta** *x10* €50-70 ℭ 987 566 431 ▯▮•*CR* **Rosalia** *x2* €45 ℭ 987 566 498. *[+0.7 km* ▯▮ •*Camping Valle do Seo* ℭ *987 566 428].* ■ **La Portela de Valcarce:** •*H¨¨* **Valcarce** *x40* €30-50 ℭ 987 543 180 N-VI. ●*Alb.* **El Peregrino** *Priv.[26÷4]* €10 *+8* €28-40 ℭ 987 543 197. ●*Alb.* **Vagabond Vieiras** *Priv.[9÷2]* €-donativo ℭ 669 329 821. ■ **Ambasmestas:** ●*Alb.* **Casa Del Pescador** *Priv.[24÷3]* €10 *+1* €22-30 ℭ 603 515 868. •*CR* **Ambasmestas** ℭ 987 233 768. •*Hs* **El Rincón del Apóstol** *x5* €17–40 ℭ 987 543 099.

● **VEGA DE VALCARCE:** ❶ **Veis** *Priv.[18÷1]* €10 *+1* ℭ 987 543 181. •*CR* **El Recanto** *x4* €50 ℭ 987 543 202. **Panadería +rooms.** ❷ **Santa María Magdalena** ℭ 684 045 491. •*CR* **Las Rocas** *x6* €35-45 ℭ 987 543 208. ❸ **Municipal.** *[64÷7]* €8 ℭ 601 501 687. •*CR* **Pandelo** *x1* €75 ℭ 987 543 033. ❹ **El Paso** *Priv.[26÷6]* €13 ℭ 628 104 309. •*P.* **Fernández** *x7* €20-35 ℭ 987 543 027. ■ **Ruitelán:** ●*Alb.* **El Rincón de PIN** *Priv.[10÷1]* ℭ 616 066 442. ●*Alb.* **Pequeño Potala** *Priv. [14÷4]* €20 media pensión ℭ 987 561. •*CR* **El Paraíso del Bierzo** ℭ 987 684 137. ■ **Herrerías:** ❶ **Las Herrerías** *Priv.[17÷3]* €7 ℭ 654 353 940. ❷ **Casa Lixa** *Priv. [30÷4]* €15 *+6* €50 ℭ 987 134 915. •*CR* **La Pandela** *x8* €40 ℭ 987 199 317.•*CR* **A Casa do Ferreiro** *x8* ℭ 987 684 903. •*CR* **Polín** *x4* ℭ 987 543 039.■ **La Faba:** ❶ **La Faba** *Asoc.[50÷3]* €8 ℭ 630 836 865. ▯▮ ❷ **Tito's** *Priv.[8÷2]* €12 ℭ 622 475 871. ■ **Laguna de Castilla:** ●*Alb.* **La Escuela** *Priv.*[*30÷5]* ℭ 987 684 786.

● **O'CEBREIRO** *Iglesia de Santa Maria Real XII. Alb.* ❶ **Casa Campelo** *Priv. [10÷1]* €15 *+4* €50 ℭ 679 678 458. *Alb.* ❷ **O'Cebreiro** *Xunta.* *[104÷2]* €8. •*H'* **O Cebreiro** *x5* €40-50 ℭ 982 367 182 •*CR* **Navarro** *x4* €30-45 ℭ 982 367 007 •*Hs* **Mesón Antón** *x4* €60+ ℭ 982 151 336 +▯▮. •*P'* **Casa Carolo** *x10* €40-48 ℭ 982 367 168. •*CR* **Venta Celta** *x5* €45+ ℭ 667 553 006 +▯▮. •*CR* **Casa Valiña** *x5* €40-50 ℭ 982 367 125. •*CR* **Casa Frade** *x5* €43 ℭ 982 367 104.

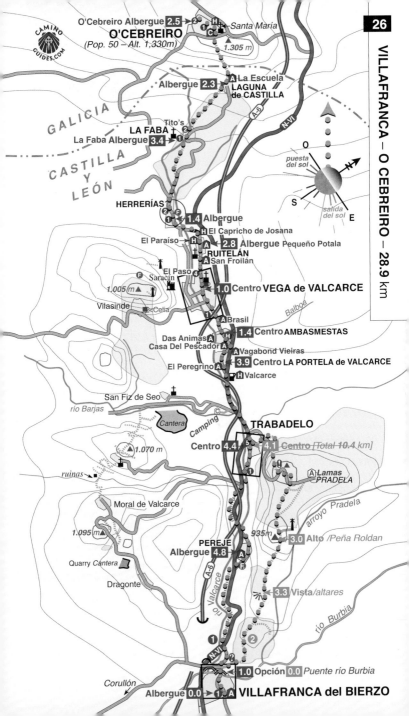

CAMINO GUIDES.COM

O'Cebreiro Albergue **2.5** ▶②
O'CEBREIRO
(Pop. 50 – Alt. 1,330m)
H **C** *Santa María*
1.305 m

GALICIA

Albergue **2.3** ▲ La Escuela
LAGUNA
de CASTILLA

CASTILLA
Y
LEÓN

Tito's †②
LA FABA
La Faba Albergue **3.4** ▶①

HERRERÍAS ②F①
1.4 Albergue
H El Capricho de Josana
El Paraíso **H** **A** **Albergue** Pequeño Potala
RUITELÁN
A San Froilán
El Paso
F Saracín
1.005 m ▲
1.0 Centro VEGA de VALCARCE
Vilasinde ■ Celia

Balboa

A Brasil
1.4 Centro AMBASMESTAS
Das Animas **A** **H**
Casa Del Pescador **A**
A Vagabond Vieiras
El Peregrino **A** **3.9 Centro LA PORTELA de VALCARCE**
□**H** Valcarce

San Fiz de Seo
río Barjas
Cantera
C Camping
TRABADELO
▲*1.070 m*
Centro 4.4 ⑤ **4.1** Centro [Total 10.4 km]
ruinas ① ①
A Lamas
PRADELA

Moral de Valcarce
arroyo Pradela
1.095 m ▲
935m ▲ **3.0 Alto** /Peña Roldan
Quarry *Cantera* ■
PEREJE
Albergue 4.8 ▶ **A**
Dragonte **F**

3.3 Vista/altares
río Burbia

río Valcarce
① ②
A-6
N-VI ①
②
1.0 Opción 0.0 *Puente río Burbia*
Corullón ◀
Albergue 0.0 ▶①**A** **VILLAFRANCA del BIERZO**

puesta del sol
O
S
E
salida del sol

27 O'CEBREIRO – TRIACASTELA

⊞⊞⊞⊞⊞⊞	--- ---	19.7 --- ---	95%
▬▬▬▬▬	--- ---	1.0 --- ---	05%
▭▭▭	--- ---	0.0	
Total km		**20.7** km *(12.9 ml)*	

Total ascent **410m** ± ¾ hr

Alto ▲ Alto do Poio **1,335**m *(4,380 ft)*

< 🅰 🏠 > ➲Liñares **3.1** km ➲Hospital **5.6** km
➲ Alto do Poio **8.6** km ➲ Fonfría **11.9** km
➲ Biduedo **14.3** km ➲ Fillobal **17.4** km.

■ **Liñares:** ●*Alb.* Linar do Rei *Priv.[20÷4]* €12 *+1* €40 ⓒ 616 464 831. •*CR* Casa Jaime *x4* €40 ⓒ 982 367 166 🍴 *bar*. ■ **Hospital de la Condesa:** ●*Alb.* Xunta.*[18÷2]* €8 ⓒ 660 396 810. O Tear 🍴/🍺. ■ **Alto do Poio:** ●*Alb.*del Puerto *Priv.[18÷1]* €6 *+4*€25 ⓒ 982 367 172. •*Hs* Santa María de Poio *x20* €40 ⓒ 982 367 167. ■ **Fonfría:** •*P* Casa Galego *x8* €40+ ⓒ 627 474 783. ●*Alb.* A Reboleira *Priv.***[50÷2]* €12 *+8* €40+ ⓒ 982 181 271. •*CR* Núñez *x2* €40 ⓒ 982 161 335. •*P* Casa Lucas *x3* €40+ ⓒ 690 346 740 *www.casadelucas.es*. ■ **Biduedo**: •*CR* Quiroga *x9* €40 ⓒ 982 187 299. •*CR* Xata *x7* €24-36 ⓒ 982 187 301. ■ **Fillobal:** ●*Alb.* Filloval *Priv.[18÷2]* €12*+2* €40 ⓒ 666 826 414.

● **TRIACASTELA:** *Alb* ❶ Xunta. *[56÷14]* €8 (photo>). •*P* García *x3* €40 ⓒ 982 548 024. ❷ Lemos *Priv.[12÷1]* €10 *+10* €43 ⓒ 677 117 238 *www. pensionalberguelemos.com* ❸ Oribio *Priv.* *[27÷2]* €10 ⓒ 982 548 085. ◀*C/ del Peregrino:* ❹ A Horta de Abel *Priv.* *[14÷2]*€11 *+3* €40 ⓒ 608 080 556. •*P* Casa Simón *x4* €40+ adj. *Igrexa de Santiago (misa del peregrino 18:00).* ❺

Atrio *Priv.[20÷4]* €10 *+6*€40 ⓒ 982 548 488 (Juan José). ❻ Complexo Xacobeo *Priv**.*[36÷3]* €11 *+12* €40 ⓒ982 548 037 adj. 🍴/🍺 *Xacobeo*. •*Hs* O'Novo ⓒ 982 548 105. ❼ Aitzenea *Priv.[38÷4]*+ €10 ⓒ 982 548 076 *www.aitzenea.com*. ❽ Berce do Camiño *Priv.[28÷6]* €9 ⓒ 982 548 127. •*P* Casa David *x7* €40 ⓒ 982 548 105 opp. •*Hs* Mesón Vilasante *x12* €35-45 ⓒ 982 548 116. •*H* Iberik *x16* €44+ ⓒ 982 650 061 *www.iberikhoteles.com* opp. •*P* Casa Pepe *x6* €50 ⓒ 622 084 338. •*CR* Olga *x4* €40+ ⓒ 982 548 134 c/ Castro 2 (+0.5 km).•*CR* Pacios €35+ ⓒ 982 548 455 Vilavella (+ 2.0 km) 🍺 *Esther* Rúa Peregrino.

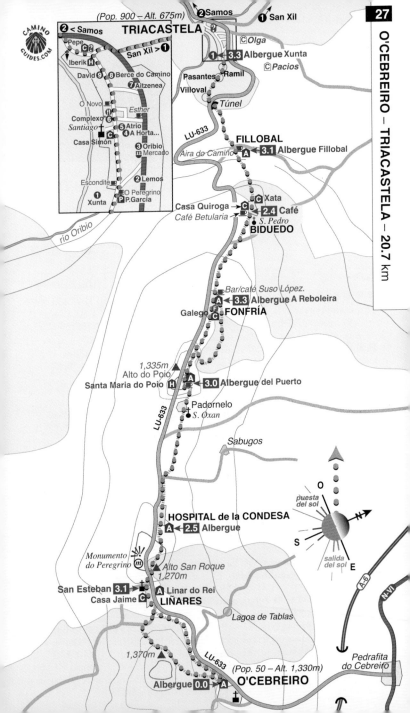

TRIACASTELA *(Pop. 900 – Alt. 675m)*

2 Samos
1 San Xil
2 < Samos

©Olga
1 **3.3** Albergue Xunta
©Pacios

Pepe ©
Iberik **H**
David **9** **8** Berce do Camiño
7 Aitzenea
O Novo
Esther
Complexo **6**
Santiago **5** Atrio
Casa Simón **4** A Horta...
3 Oribio
Mercado
Escondite
O Peregrino **2** Lemos
P P.García
1 Xunta
rio Oribio

San Xil **1**

Pasantes   Ramil
Villoval
Túnel

LU-633

FILLOBAL
Aira do Camiño **A** **3.1** Albergue Fillobal

©Xata
Casa Quiroga → **C**
Café Betularia → **2.4** Café
S. Pedro
BIDUEDO

Bar/café Suso López.
A **3.3** Albergue A Reboleira
Galego **C** **FONFRÍA**

1,335m
Alto do Poio
Santa Maria do Poio **H** **A** **3.0** Albergue del Puerto

Padornelo
S. Oxan

Sabugos

HOSPITAL de la CONDESA
A **2.5** Albergue

Monumento do Peregrino **m**
Alto San Roque
1,270m
San Esteban **3.1** **A** Linar do Rei
Casa Jaime **C** **LIÑARES**

Lagoa de Tablas

1,370m

LU-633   *(Pop. 50 – Alt. 1,330m)*

Albergue **0.0** **A** **O'CEBREIRO**

Pedrafita do Cebreiro

A-6
NVI

O
puesta del sol
N
S
E
salida del sol

28 TRIACASTELA – SARRIA

⣿⣿⣿⣿⣿	--- --- 11.2 --- ---	60%
▬▬▬▬▬	--- --- 7.5 --- ---	40%
▬▬▬	--- --- 0.0	
Total km	**18.7** km *(11.6 ml)*	

Total ascent **230**m ± ½ *hr*
Alto ▲ Alto do Riocabo **905**m *(2,970 ft)*
< 🅰 🅷 > ➊ *San Xil:* ➲🅰 Balsa **1.6** km
➲Pintín **12.1** km ➲ Calvor **13.4** km ➲Vigo de Sarria **17.7** km
➋ *Samos:* ➲*Lusío 5.1 km* (+ 0.4) ➲ Samos **10.5** km ➲ San Mamed **21.4** km

➊ ● ● ● ●▮**A Balsa:** ●*Alb.* Ecologico El Beso *Priv.[16÷3]* €10 *V.* ☏ 633 550
558. **Montán Fontearcuda** *[Mondaviega Alquimista].*▮ **Pintín:** •*P¨*Casa Cines *x7*
€35+ ☏ 982 090 837. ▮ **Calvor:** ●*Alb.* Calvor *Xunta.[22÷2]* €8 ☏ 982 531 266.

➋ ● ● ● /○ *Lusío* + 400m: ●*Alb.* Forte
de Lusío *Xunta.[60÷4]* €8 ☏ 659 721 324.
● **SAMOS:** ➊ Val de Samos *Priv.[52÷7]*
€12 ☏ 982 546 163. ➋ Monasterio de
Samos *Conv.[66÷1]* €-donativo ☏982 546
046 *(misa del peregrino 19:30).* ➌ Externa
Monasterio €12 *x30* €25-40 ☏ 643 639 226.
➍ Tras do Convento *Priv.[10÷1]* €12 +2
€25 ☏ 982 546 051. •Casas de Outeiro
spa €85 ☏ 680 379 969. •*P* Casa da Botica
x14 €45+ ☏ 982 546 095. •*P* Santa Rosa
x4 ☏633 430 219. •*CR* Licerio *x5* €35+ ☏
982 546 145. •*Hs* A Veiga *x15* €40+ ☏ 982
546 052. ▮ **Gorolfe:** •*H* Casa de Díaz *x12*
€39+ ☏ 982 547 070 ▮ **Sivil:** •*P* A Fonte
das Bodas *x4* €40 ☏982 099 103

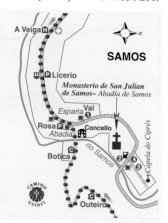

SAMOS

▮ **S. Mamede del Camino:** ▲ Vila de Sarria €25 ☏ 982 535 467. •*P¨* Ana *x6* €30
☏ 982 531 458. 🍴 *Meson Casa Silva*

● **VIGO DE SARRIA:** ➊ *Turismo* ☏ 982 530 099 (albergues ±€12) ➍ A Pedra
Priv.*[23÷5]+4 ☏ 982 530 130. ➑ **Oasis** *Priv.[27÷4]* ☏ 982 535 516 adj. •*P¨*
Siete *x6* €35+ ☏ 982 044 208. •*Hs* Cristal *x15* €45 ☏ 669 799 512. 🍴/☕ Barullo
Priv[20÷1]+2 Praza de Galicia, 40. ➍ Credencial *Priv. [28÷2]* ☏ 982 876 455
Rúa do Peregrino, 50-bajo. ➋Alma do Camiño *Priv.[100÷10]* ☏ 982 876 768
•*P¨*Blasones *x14* €20-40 ☏ 652 256 226 c/ Ameneirizas. •*H¨¨¨¨* Alfonso IX *x60*
€60+ ☏ 982 530 005 •*P* Rúa Peregrino *x11* €50 ☏ 982 886 662. ➎ Puente
Ribeira *Priv.[28÷3]*+8 ☏ 982 876 789 Rúa do Peregrino, Nº 23

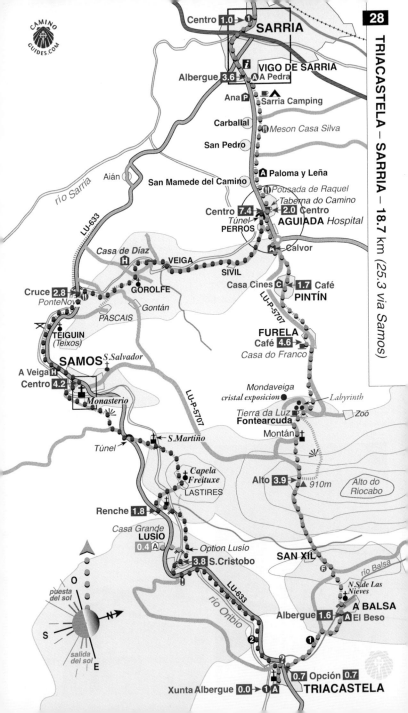

Centro **1.0** ➊ **SARRIA**

ℹ️ **VIGO DE SARRIA**

Albergue **3.6** Ⓐ A Pedra

Ana 🅿️ ⛺ Sarria Camping

Carballal

🍴 *Meson Casa Silva*

San Pedro

Ⓐ Paloma y Leña

San Mamede del Camino

🍴 *Pousada de Raquel*
Taberna do Camino
Centro **7.4** Centro **2.0** Centro
Túnel **AGUIADA** *Hospital*
PERROS

Ⓐ Calvor

río Sarria

Aián

Casa de Díaz
Ⓗ **VEIGA**
SIVIL

Cruce **2.8** 🍴
PonteNov
GOROLFE
Gontán
PASCAIS

Casa Cines Ⓒ **1.7** Café
PINTÍN

LU-633

LU-P-5707

FURELA
Café **4.6** ➔
Casa do Franco

✗ **TEIGUIN**
(Teixos)
SAMOS S.Salvador

Mondaveiga
cristal exposicion ● *Labyrinth*
Tierra da Luz Ⓢ *Zoó*
Fontearcuda
Montán ✝

A Veiga Ⓗ
Centro **4.2** ✝
Monasterio

LU-P-5707

Túnel ✝ *S.Martiño*

Alto **3.9** ▲ 910m *Alto do Riocabo*

✝ *Capela Freituxe*
LASTIRES

Renche **1.8** ➔ ✝

Casa Grande
LUSIO
0.4 Ⓐ
Option Lusío
3.8 S.Cristobo

SAN XIL

Ⓕ *río Balsa*

río Oribio
LU-633
N.S.de Las Nieves
✝ **A BALSA**
Albergue **1.6** Ⓐ El Beso

O
puesta del sol
S
N
E
salida del sol

➋ ➊

0.7 Opción **0.7**
Xunta Albergue **0.0** ➊Ⓐ ✝ **TRIACASTELA**

● **SARRIA** *Centro [km. 111,5]* ◖**Rúa Maior.** ❶ – ⑯ (Av. price €12):
❶ **Casa Peltre** *Priv [22÷3]* ⓒ 606 226 067. •*P*˙Escalinata *x8* €40 ⓒ 982 530 259. ◖**Rúa Maior Nº64** ❷ Mayor. *Priv.[16÷3]* ⓒ 685 148 474. **Nº79** ❸ **Xunta** *[40÷1]* ⓒ 660 396 813 (€8). **Nº62** •*P*˙˙Aqua *x3* €45 ⓒ 620 988 251. **Nº44** ❹ **O Durmiñento** *Priv.[38÷5]+1* ⓒ 982 531 099 roof terrace. **Nº53** •*P*˙˙˙Casa Barán *x4* €75 ⓒ 982 876 487. **Nº57** ❺ **Internacional** *Priv.[38÷4]+2* ⓒ 982 535 109 roof terrace. **Nº49** ❻ **Obradoiro** *Priv.[38÷2]* ⓒ 982 532 442 garden terrace. **Nº31** ❼ **Los Blasones** *Priv.*˙*[42÷4]* ⓒ 600 512 565 rear patio. **Nº29** ❽ **El Bordón** *Priv.[6÷4] +4* ⓒ 982 530 652. **Nº19** •*P*˙ Mesón Camino Francés ⓒ 982 532 351 (opp. Mesón O Tapas). **Nº10** ❾ **Don Álvaro** *Priv.[40÷6]+7* ⓒ 982 531 592 rear patio. **Nº4** ❿ **Matías** *Priv.[30÷1]+6* ⓒ 982 534 285 adj. ⑪ *Matias Locanda Italiana.* •*H*˙˙Nova *x17* €40+ ⓒ 982 605 021, pl. Constitución, 4. ⓫ **Sleeping Sarria** *Priv.* 16 beds in shared rooms of up to 4 people ⓒ 689 319 941 c/Esqueirodos,1. ⓬**Monasterio de la Magdalena** *Priv.[110÷5]* Av. de la Merced, ⓒ 982 533 568 'twinned' with albergue Seminario Menor in Santiago. ⓭ **San Lázaro** *Priv.[27÷3]+4* ⓒ 982 530 626 c/San Lázaro,7. •*P* La Casona de Sarria *x6* €50 ⓒ 982 535 556 Rúa San Lázaro 24. ⓮ **Andaina** *Priv.[26÷2]* ⓒ 628 232 103 Rúa Calvo Sotelo, 11.•*P*˙La Estación *x5* €30 ⓒ 658 094 994 c/ Matías López,106. •*P*Matias Rooms *x10* €35+ Calle Rosalia de Castro, 19 ⓒ 982 534 285). •*P*˙ Casa Matías *x10* €26 ⓒ 659 160 498 Calvo Sotelo,39. •*H*˙ Mar de Plata *x25* €50+ ⓒ 982 530 724. Adj. railway station •*Hr*˙ Roma ⓒ 982 532 211 Calvo Sotelo,2.

◖**Pilgrim equipment:** •*Peregrinoteca* c/ Benigno Quiroga, 16 (08:00–20:00) ⓒ 982 530 190 •*Xesta* c/José Sánachez Arias •*Kilometr 112* rua do Peregrino,37.

Monumentos Históricos: ❶ *Iglesia de Santa Mariña XIX (credenciales y misa del peregrino 18:00).* ❷ *Iglesia del Salvador XIII.* ❸ *Hospital de San Anton XVI (antiguo hospital de peregrino).* ❹ *Fortaleza de Sarria y Torres XIII (ruinas).* ❺ *Monasterio de Santa María Madalena XIII (Convento de la Merced. Credenciales y misa del peregrino 18:30).*

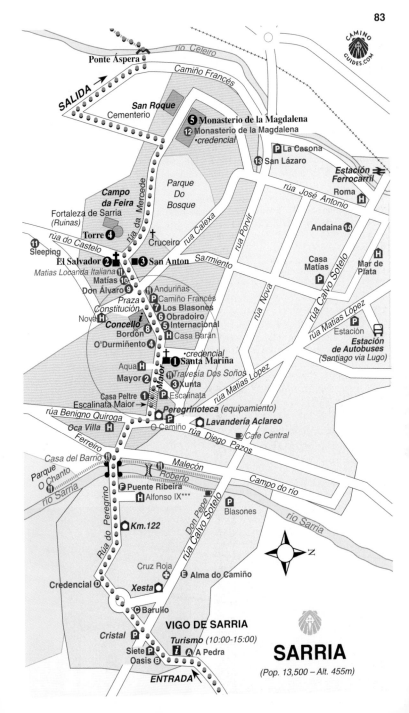

Ponte Áspera

río Celeiro

SALIDA

Camiño Francés

San Roque
Cementerio

5 Monasterio de la Magdalena
12 Monasterio de la Magdalena
•credencial

P La Casona

13 San Lázaro

Estación Ferrocarril

rúa José Antonio

Roma **H**

Campo da Feira

Fortaleza de Sarria
(Ruinas)

Torre 4

rúa do Castelo

11 Sleeping

Parque Do Bosque

rúa da Mercede

Cruceiro

rúa Calexa

Sarmiento

rúa Porvir

Andaina **14**

Casa Matías **P**

H Mar de Plata

rúa Calvo Sotelo

El Salvador 2 **H** San Anton **3**

Matías Locanda Italiana **H**
Matías **10**
Don Álvaro **9**

Anduriñas
P Camiño Francés
7 Los Blasones
6 Obradoiro
5 Internacional
H Casa Barán

Praza Constitución
Nova **H**
Concello **i**
Bordón **8**
O'Durmiñento **4**

rúa Nova

rúa Matías López

P Estación

Estación de Autobuses
(Santiago via Lugo)

•credencial

1 Santa Mariña

Aqua **H**
Mayor **2**

Casa Peltre **1**
Escalinata Maior →

rúa Benigno Quiroga

Travesía Dos Soños **H**
3 Xunta
P Escalinata

rúa Matías López

Peregrinoteca (equipamiento)

H Lavandería Aclareo

Oca Villa **H**
O Camiño
rúa Diego Pazos
P Cafe Central

Ferreiro

Casa del Barrio **H**

Malecón

Roberto **H**

Campo do río

Parque O Chanto

río Sarria

F Puente Ribeira
H Alfonso IX***

P Blasones

río Sarria

Km.122

rúa do Peregrino

Don Pepe

rúa Calvo Sotelo

N

Cruz Roja
E Alma do Camiño

Credencial **D**

Xesta

C Barullo

VIGO DE SARRIA

Cristal **P**

Turismo (10:00-15:00)

Siete **P**
Oasis **B**
i **A** Pedra

ENTRADA

SARRIA
(Pop. 13,500 – Alt. 455m)

29 SARRIA – PORTOMARÍN

....	--- --- 11.4 --- ---	*50%*
▬▬▬	--- --- 10.7 --- ---	*48%*
▬▬▬	--- --- 0.6 --- ---	*2%*
Total km	**22.7** km	(*14.1 ml*)

Total ascent **940m** ± *1½ hr*

Alto ▲ Alto Momientos **660m** (*2,165 ft*)

<**A H**> ● Barbadelo ❶ **3.7** km – ❺ **4.5** km.
● Morgade **12.4** km. ● Ferreiros **13.8** ● Mercadoiro **17.3** ● Vilacha **20.4** km.

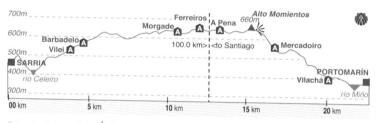

■ **Barbadelo** *Vilei:* 🏠/❶ Casa Barbadelo *Priv.[48÷6]* €12 +*11* €50 ✆ 982 531
934. ❷.**108 km** *Priv.[14÷5]*+ €8-15 ✆ 634 894 524 ***cerrado?*** ❸ O Pombal *Priv.*
[12÷1] €12 ✆ 686 718 732 (+200m). ❹Barbadelo *Xunta.[18÷2]* €6 ✆ 660 396
814. ❺ Casa de Carmen *Priv.*[24÷3]*+ €11 (+€35) ✆ 982 532 294 ✆ 982
532 294. ■ **Rente:** •*CR* Casanova *x6* ✆ 982 187 854. ■ **Peruscallo:** ● Molino
de Marzán *Priv.[14÷1]* €12 ✆ 679 438 077. ■ **Morgade** ● Casa Morgade *Priv.*
[6÷1]€12 +*13* €40 ✆ 982 531 250. ■ **Ferreiros:** 🍴/❶ Casa Cruceiro *Priv.[24÷2]*
€12 +*2* €50 ✆982 541 240 *www.casacruceirodeferreiros.com*. ❷ Ferreiros *Xunta.*
[22÷1] €8 ✆ 982 157 496. ■ **Mercadoiro:** ● Mercadoiro *Priv.[22÷3]*€12 +*4* €45
✆ 982 545 359.+ 🍴/🏠 *Bodeguiña* ■ **Vilachá:** ●*Alb.* Casa Banderas *[9÷1]* €13 +*1*
€40 ✆ 682 179 589. ●*Alb.* Vilachá *[10÷1]* €13 ✆ 696 004 491. ■ **Loio** +*1.9 km*
•*H Meson do Loyo x9* €40+ ✆ 982 545 012.

● **PORTOMARÍN** *p.86*

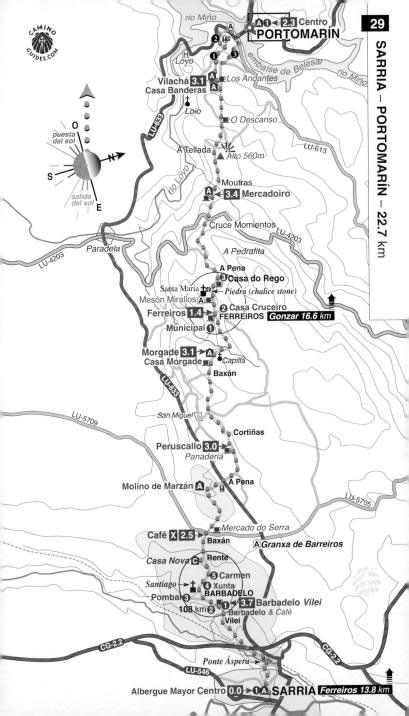

rio Miño

▲1 ◀ 2.3 Centro
PORTOMARÍN

embalse de Belesar

rio Miño

Ⓗ Loyo

Vilachá 3.1
Casa Banderas

Los Andantes

Loio

O Descanso

A Tellada
▲ *Alto 560m*

Moutras

▲ ◀ 3.4 **Mercadoiro**

LU-613

Cruce Momientos LU-4203

A Pedrafita

A Pena
❸*Casa do Rego*
Santa Maria ✝ ← *Piedra (chalice stone)*
Mesón Mirallos ▲
Ferreiros 1.4 ❷ *Casa Cruceiro*
FERREIROS *Gonzar 16.6 km*
Municipal ❶

Morgade 3.1 ▲
Casa Morgade ✝*Capilla*

Baxán

LU-633

San Miguel

LU-5709

LU-4203

Paradela

rio Loyo

Cortiñas

Peruscallo 3.0
Panaderia

A Pena

Molino de Marzán ▲ ₪

Mercado do Serra LU-5705

Café ✕ 2.5
Baxán
▲*Granxa de Barreiros*
Casa Nova Ⓒ
Rente
❺ *Carmen*
Santiago ✝ ❹ *Xunta*
BARBADELO
Pombal ❸ ❶ 3.7 **Barbadelo** *Vilei*
108 km ❷ *Barbadelo & Café*
Vilei

Ponte Áspera →

CG-2.2

LU-546

Albergue Mayor Centro 0.0 ▶ ❶▲ **SARRIA** *Ferreiros 13.8 km*

O
puesta del sol
S
N
E
salida del sol

● **PORTOMARÍN:** ◀*Albergues:* ❶Casona de Ponte *Priv.[47÷5]* €12 *+16* €50+ Ⓒ 982 169 862 <u>www.casonadaponte.com</u> c/Capela. ❷Pons Minea *Priv. [24÷3] +6* €40+ Ⓒ 610 737 995 Av. Sarria. ❸Ferramenteiro *Priv.*[130÷1]* €10 Ⓒ 982 545 362 c/Chantada. ❹Folgueira *Priv.[32÷1]* €12 Ⓒ 982 545 166 Av. Chantada. ❺Aqua *Priv.[10÷1]* €12 *+3* €35+ Ⓒ 608 921 372 c/Barreiros. ❻Casa Cruz *Priv.[16÷1]* €12 Ⓒ 982 545 140 *c/Benigno Quiroga* Nº16 &@ Nº12 ❼Novo Porto *Priv.[22÷1]* €12 Ⓒ 982 545 277. ❽El Caminante *Priv.[12÷4]* +15 €30+ Ⓒ 982 545 176 c/Sánchez Carro, 7. ❾Ultreia *Priv.*[14÷1]* +5 €35+ Ⓒ 982 545 067 *c/Diputación* Nº9 opp. Nº8 ❿Porto Santiago *Priv.*[7÷1]*€15 +5 €40+Ⓒ 618 826 515 *+4* €25-35. ⓫Pasiño a Pasiño *Priv.[30÷6]* €12 Ⓒ 665 667 243 r/ Compostela 25. ⓬Huellas *Priv.[6÷1]* €12 *+3* €35+ Ⓒ 681 398 278 r/Peregrino Nº15. ⓭Villamartín *Priv.[22÷2]* €15 Ⓒ 982 545 054. ⓮Portomarín *Xunta. [86÷6]* €8 Ⓒ 660 396 816. ⓯ Manuel *Priv.[16÷2]* €10 *+4* €25 Ⓒ 982 545 385 c/ Miño 1. ⓰Casa do Marabillas *Priv.[16÷4]* €14 *+2* €30+ Ⓒ 744 450 425 c/Monte.

◀*Hoteles:*•P Gonzar *[12÷1]* €12x6 €30+ Ⓒ 982 545 275 + bar. •H⁺Ferramenteiro *x22* €55-80 Ⓒ 982 545 361. •Spa H¨ Vistalegre *x20* €80+ Ⓒ 982 545 076 *c/ Compostela* Nº29 &@Nº10 •P¨Casa S. Nicolas *x12* €55+ Ⓒ 669 497 243 <u>www. casasannicolas.es</u> ◀*Centro: Praza Conde Fenosa* •P¨¨Arenas Ⓒ 982 545 386. •H¨ Villajardín *x36* €40-70 Ⓒ 982 545 054 <u>www.hotelvillajardin.com</u> r/Miño 14. •P¨¨Casa do Maestro *x10* €50-70 Ⓒ 626 510 806 <u>www.casadomaestro.com</u> adj. S.Xoan on *r/Fraga Iribarne* Nº1 &@ Nº5 •P¨ Mar *x8* €34-40 Ⓒ 622 611 211 &@ Nº18 •Hs¨El Padrino (*Mirador*) *x6* €60-70 Ⓒ 982 545 323. •H⁺Pazo de Berbetoros *Marquesa x3* €60+ Ⓒ 982 545 292 r/San Pedro. •P Pérez *x10* €35+ Ⓒ 982 545 040 Pl. A. Española. •P Baires *[5÷1]* €15 *+3* €30+ Ⓒ 645 118 958. ◀*Alto:* •P˙ Portomiño *x24* €35+ Ⓒ 982 547 575 <u>www.portomino.com</u> c/Sánchez Carro, 23 (◀ *Portomiño*). •P Ribeira Sacra *x4* €30-50 Ⓒ 608 921 372 Camiño do v. •P¨¨Posada *x34* €55-77 Ⓒ 982 545 200.

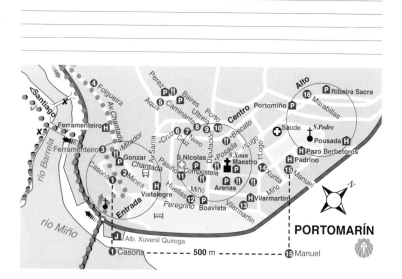

PORTOMARÍN

● **PALAS de REI:** ❶ *Turismo* Av. de Compostela 28 © 982 380 001

◀*Entrada:* ❶Os Chacotes *Xunta.* *[112÷3]* €8 © 607 481 536. •*H¨¨*Complejo La Cabana *x30* €45-59 © 982 380 750. *Centro:* (albergues Av. €10) ❷Mesón de Benito *Priv.[78÷6]* © 982 103 386. ❸Zendoira *Priv.[50÷2]* +6 €30+ © 629727605 Amado Losada 10 (off Av.Ourense). •*Hs* O Castelo *x8* €45+

© 618 401 130. ☂/•*P* O Cruceiro *x10* €45+ © 649 629 725. •*Hs* Mica *x16* €50+ © 689 339 770 and •*P* Casa Curro *x8* €40 (1). ❹Outeiro *Priv.[60÷8]* © 982 380 242 adj. Plaza de Galicia. ❺San Marcos *Priv.[60÷10]+20* © 982 380 711 *www.alberguesanmarcos.es*. ❻ Castro *Priv.***[60÷9]* © 609 080 655 on corner. •*Hr¨*Benilde *x7* © 982 380 717 r/Mercado •*P* Pardellas © 982 380 181.

◀*Centro:* ❼Xunta *[60÷5]* €8 *Av. Compostela* **Nº19**. @**Nº24** •*P* Fonte *x10* €50 © 671 231 991 *www.pensionafonte. com* @**Nº16** ❽*Alb/P¨*Arenas Palas *Priv.* *[24÷4]* €4 +15 €35-50 © 982 380 326

+*250m* •*P* Cabalo Verde *x25* €25-50 © 679 911 186 Trv/Feira +*500m* •*P* Palas *x15* €40+ © 982 380 065 c/S.Tirso. ✚ *down (left)* @**Nº21** ☂ *bar*/•*P* Plaza *x14* €25-45 © 660 875 921 adj. *Travesía del Peregrino*. @**Nº10** •*P* Casa Camiño *x15* €40-55 © 982 374 066 (+ Casa Camiño II @**Nº8**). •*P¨¨*As Hortas *x7* €59-79 © 626 518 388 *www.pensionashortas.com* r/Hortas ❾ BuenCamino *Priv.***[42÷8]* © 982 380 233. A +*300m:* ❿A Casiña di Marcello *Priv.[16÷2]* © 640 723 903 c/Camiño de abaixo. +*1km* •*Hs* Ponterroxán *x18* €25-30 © 982 380 132.

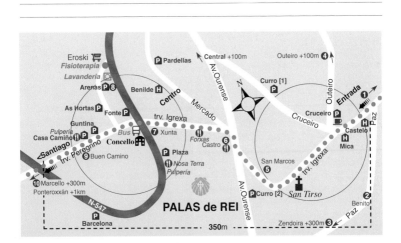

30 PORTOMARÍN – PALAS DE REI

```
--- --- 19.8 --- --- 80%
--- --- 4.8 --- --- 20%
--- --- 0.0
Total km 24.6 km (15.3 ml)
```

Total ascent **1,050**m ± *1¾ hr*
Alto ▲ Sierra Ligonde **720**m (*2,362 ft*)
< Ⓐ Ⓗ > ➲ Gonzar 7.7 km ➲ Hospital **11.0**
➲ Ventas de Narón **12.6** km ➲ Ligonde **16.3**
➲ Eirexe **16.9** km ➲ Portos **19.1** km ➲ Os Chacotes **23.4** km.

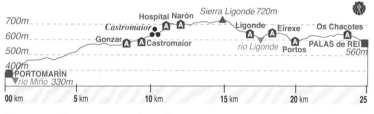

■ **Gonzar:** ❶Hostería *Priv.[20÷2]* €12 *+13* €40+ ℂ 982 154 878 *www.hosteriadegonzar.com*. ❷ Gonzar *Xunta.[28÷1]* €8 ℂ 982 157 840. ❸ Casa Garcia *Priv.[26÷2]* €10 *+4* €35 ℂ 982 157 842 (+100m). ☏/●*Alb.* Ortiz *Priv.[12÷1]* €10 *+4* €40 ℂ 982 099 416. ■ **Castromaior** •*P* Casa Maruja *x4* €16+ ℂ 982 189 054. •*P* Perdigueira *x4* €40+ ℂ 690 852 026. ■ **Hospital de la Cruz:** •*Hs* El Labrador €30+ ℂ 982 545 303. ●*Alb.* Hospital de la Cruz *Xunta.[32÷2]* €8. ■ **Ventas de Narón:** *Alb.*❶ Casa Molar *Priv.[18÷2]* €10 *+2* €30 ℂ 696 794 507. *Alb.*❷ O Cruceiro *Priv.***[26÷3]* €12 *+6* €30 ℂ 658 064 917. ■ **Ligonde:** •*CR* Tania *x3* €60-120 ℂ 604 047 316. *Alb.*❶ Fuente del Peregrino *Asoc.[9÷2]* €-donativo ℂ 687 550 527. ❷ Escuela de Ligonde *Muni.[20÷1]* €8 ℂ 982 153 483. ■ **Airexe:** ●*Alb.* Airexe *Xunta.[20÷2]* €8. •*P* Eirexe *x5* €25-50 ℂ 982 153 475. ■ **Portos:** ●*Alb.* A Paso de Formiga (Ants Way!) *Priv.[12÷2]* €13 *+2* €50 ℂ 618 984 605. ■ **Lestedo:** ⅃/•*CR*. Rectoral de Lestedo *x7* €80+ ℂ 982 153 435.

● **PALAS de REI** *p.87*

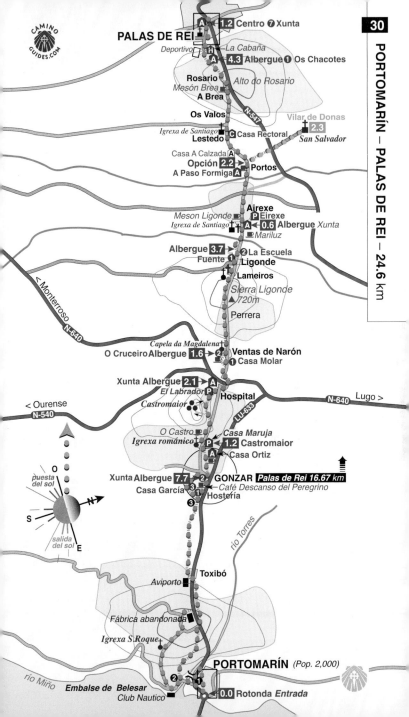

CAMINO
GUIDES.COM

PALAS DE REI ■ A■ **1.2** Centro ❼ Xunta

Deportivo □ ᛏ Ⓗ *La Cabaña*
□ A■ **4.3** Albergue ❶ Os Chacotes

Rosario ■
Mesón Brea
A Brea ■

Os Valos ■

Igrexa de Santiago ᛏ ■ *Vilar de Donas* ᛏ **2.3**
Lestedo Ⓒ Casa Rectoral *San Salvador*

Casa A Calzada A■
Opción 2.2 ►►
A Paso Formiga A■ ►► Portos

Airexe P Eirexe
Meson Ligonde ■■ ᛏ
Igrexa de Santiago ᛏ■ A■ **0.6** Albergue *Xunta*
Mariluz

Albergue **3.7** ► ❷ La Escuela
Fuente ❶ **Ligonde** ■

ᛏᛏ **Lameiros**

Sierra Ligonde
▲720m

Perrera

Capela da Magdalena ᛏ
O Cruceiro Albergue **1.6** ► ❷ **Ventas de Narón**
❶ Casa Molar

Xunta Albergue **2.1** ► A■
El Labrador P
Castromaior ■ **Hospital**

O Castro ■ *Casa Maruja*
Igrexa románico ᛏ P **1.2** Castromaior
A■ Casa Ortiz

Xunta Albergue **7.7** ► ❷ **GONZAR** Palas de Rei 16.67 km
Casa García ❸ ❶ ← *Café Descanso del Peregrino*
❸ Hostería

río Torres

■ **Toxibó**
Aviporto ■

Fábrica abandonada ◆

Igrexa S.Roque ᛏ

PORTOMARÍN *(Pop. 2,000)*

río Miño ❷ ᕁ ❶
Embalse de Belesar
Club Nautico ■ □ **0.0** Rotonda *Entrada*

< Monterroso
N-640

< Ourense
N-540

N-540
N-547

Vilar de Donas
N-547

N-640 Lugo >

LU-633

O
*puesta
del sol*
N
S
E
*salida
del sol*

Alto do Rosario

31 PALAS DE REI – RIBADISO (ARZÚA)

·············· --- --- 18.9 --- ---	72%
▬▬▬ --- --- 6.6 --- --- 25%	
▬▬▬ --- --- 0.8 --- --- 3%	
Total km **26.3** km (*16.3 ml*)	

▲ Total ascent **820**m ± 1¼ *hr*
Alto ▲ O Coto **515**m (*1,670 ft*)
< 🅰 🅗 > ➲ San Xulián **3.6** km ➲ Casanova **5.9** km ➲ O Coto **8.7** km
➲ Melide **15.1** km ➲ Boente **21.0** km ➲ Castañeda **23.2** km.

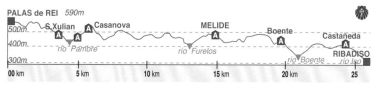

■ **San Xulián (*Xiao*) do Camiño:** ●*Alb.* O Abrigadoiro *Priv.[18÷3]* €12 ℰ 982 374 117. •*CR* La Pallota *x4* €70+ ℰ 659 070 510. ■ **Ponte Campaña-Mato:** ●*Alb.* Casa Domingo *Priv.***[21÷3]* €14 ℰ 982 163 226. ■ **Casanova:** ●*Alb.* Mato Casanova *Xunta. [20÷1]* €8 ℰ 982 173 483. ● *Vilar de Remonde: (+1½ km)* •*CR* Bolboreta *x8* €40+ ℰ 609 124 717. ■ **O Coto** •*P¨* Los dos Alemanes *x14* €25-€50 ℰ 630 910 803. •*CR¨*Casa de los Somoza *x10* €45+ ℰ 981 507 372. ■ **Furelos** •*P¨¨*Adro *x3* €85.

● **MELIDE** *p.92*

■ **Penas** •*CR* Ponte de Penas *x10* €75+ ℰ 981 501 163 *www.casadapontedepenas.com*
■ **Boente Arriba:** •*H* Rectoral de Boente *x8* €85 ℰ 684 238 323. ●*Alb.* El Alemán *[40÷4]* €16 ℰ 981 501 984. ■ **Boente** *Igrexa Santiago*: *Alb.*❶ Boente *Priv.[42÷4]* €14 +*6*€40+ ℰ 981 501 974 + menú. ❷ Fuente Saleta *Priv.[22÷6]* €12 ℰ 981 501 853 + menú. ■ **Castañeda:** ●*Alb.* Santiago *Priv.* *[4÷1]* €13 +*1*40 ℰ 981 501 711. •*App* La Calleja ℰ 605 787 382 from €80. ●*(+400m / N-547)* •*CR Garea x6* €50 ℰ *981 500 400* + •*Milía x8* €35+ ℰ *981 515 241*.

● **Ribadiso da Baixo:** *Alb.*❶ Ribadiso *Xunta.[60÷2]* €8 ℰ 660 396 823. ❷ Los Caminantes *Priv.[68÷4]* €10 +*9* €30+ ℰ 647 020 600 *www.albergueloscaminantes. com*. •*P* Ribadiso €59+ ℰ 981 500 703.

 +**0.9** km ●*Alb.* Milpes *Priv.[24÷2]* €12 ℰ 981 500 425 (+0.9 km). ●*Alb.* Miraiso *Priv.[10÷2]*+ €12 ℰ 722 297 498

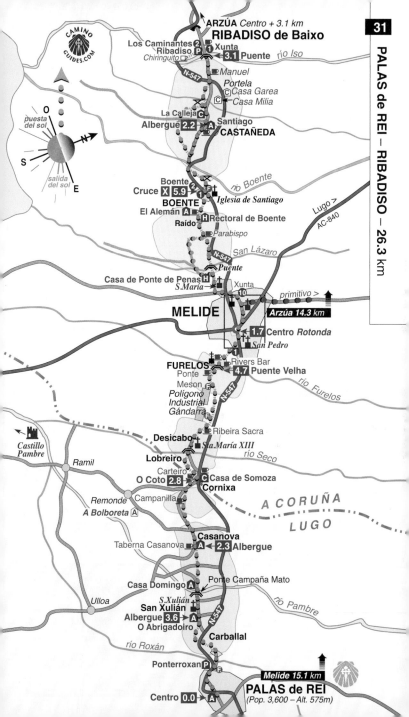

ARZÚA *Centro + 3.1 km*
RIBADISO de Baixo
Los Caminantes
Ribadiso
Chiringuito
Xunta
3.1 Puente *río Iso*

Manuel
Portela
Casa Garea
Casa Milia
La Calleja
Albergue **2.2** Santiago
CASTAÑEDA

río Boente
Boente
Cruce **5.9**
BOENTE
Iglesia de Santiago
El Alemán
Raído **Rectoral de Boente**
Parabispo
San Lázaro
N-547
Lugo >
AC-840

Puente
Casa de Ponte de Penas
S.María
Xunta
MELIDE
primitivo >
Arzúa 14.3 km

1.7 Centro *Rotonda*
San Pedro

Rivers Bar
FURELOS
Ponte **4.7** Puente Velha
Meson
Polígono
Industrial
Gándara
río Furelos

Ribeira Sacra
Desicabo
Sta.María XIII
Lobreiro
río Seco

Castillo Pambre
Ramil
Carteiro
O Coto **2.8** Casa de Somoza
Cornixa
Remonde
Campanilla
A Bolboreta
A CORUÑA
LUGO

Casanova
Taberna Casanova **2.3** Albergue

Casa Domingo
Ponte Campaña Mato
Ulloa
S.Xulián
San Xulián
Albergue **3.6**
O Abrigadoiro
río Pambre
N-547
Carballal
río Roxán

Ponterroxan
Melide 15.1 km

Centro **0.0**
PALAS de REI
(Pop. 3,600 – Alt. 575m)

● **MELIDE:** *Pop.7,500* ❶ *Turismo* (9:00-15:00) Plaza Convento © 981 505 003.

(Albergues Av. €12) ❶Melide *Priv.[40÷2]* © 627 901 552 *www.alberguemelide. com* Av. Lugo. •*H¨***Carlos** *x34* €25-55 © 981 507 633. Keep s/o past •*CR* **A Lua do Camiño** *x8* €25-35 © 6620 958 331 and ❚❙ *Casa Alongas V.* ❷**Ezequiel** *Priv. [18÷3]* © 686 583 378 r/Sol,7. •*Hs¨***Xaneiro** *x26* €45 © 981 506 140 Av. de la Habana,43. •*P* **El Molino** *x8* €25+ © 981 506 048 c/Rosalía de Castro, 23. ❸ **Arraigos** *Priv.[24÷1]* © 646 343 370 Cantón de San Roque •*P¨* **Berenguela** *x12* €30-40 © 981 505 417.

◀*Centro* ❹ O Cruceiro *Priv.[80÷12]* © 616 764 896 *www.albergueocruceiro. es.* ❺ O Candil *Priv.[12÷2]* €15 © 639 503 550 *www.ocandil.gal.*•*P* Esquina *x12* €40+ © 981 505 802 c/Ichoas, 1. ❻ Alfonso II *El Casto Priv.[30÷3]*+ © 981 506 454 *www.alberguealfonsoelcasto.com* Av. de Toques y Friol 52 (AC-840). ◀*Rua S.Antonio:* @N°6 ❼ San Antón *Priv.[36÷5]* © 981 506 427 *www. alberguesananton.com* @N°14 •*P* San Antón *x 12* €35-50 © 698 153 672 @N°18 •*Pousada* Chiquitín *x 16* €30-50 © 981 815 333 *www.chiquitinmelide.es.* @N°23 ❽ O Apalpador *Priv.[12÷2]* © 679 837 969 adj. ❾ Melide *Xunta.[140÷6]* €8 © 660 396 822. *N-547 Rua Progreso/ Codeseira* ❿ Pereiro *Priv.[40÷5]* +4 €40 © 981 506 314. ⓫ **Montoto** *Priv.[50÷4]* +1 €30 © 646 941 887 *www. alberguemontoto.com.* •*P* Sony *x30* €40+ © 981 505 473. *(AC-840)* •*P* Orois *x12* €40 © 981 507 097 c/A. Boveda, 13. ❚❙•*P.* ♥ O Tobo do Lobo *x10* €35+ © 981 507 773 c/Luis Seoane, 8.

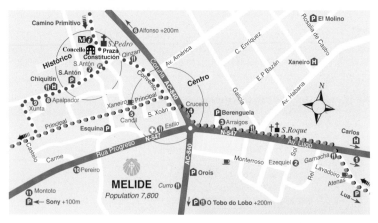

● **PEDROUZO:** *Albergues Av.€12-€15:*

❶ **O Burgo** *Priv.*[14÷1]+5* €40 © 630 404 138 *www.albergueoburgo.es*. ❷ **Arca** *Xunta.[150÷4].* ❸ **Mirador** *[50÷7]* €15 © 686 871 215 *www. alberguemiradordepedrouzo.com Centro:* ❹ **Porta de Santiago** *Priv.*[54÷2]* © 981 511 103 *www.portadesantiago. com*  ❺ **O Trisquel** *Priv.[78÷6]* © 616 644 740 Rúa do Picon. ❻ **Edreira** *Priv.*[40÷4]* © 981 511 365 *www. albergue-edreira.com* Rúa da Fonte 19. ❼ **REMhostel** *Priv.[50÷2]* © 981 510 407. Adj. ❽ **Cruceiro** *Priv.[94÷6]* © 981 511 371 *www.albergue cruceirodepedrouzo. com* Av. Iglesia. ❾ **Otero** *Priv.[34÷2]* © 671 663 374 *www.albergueotero.com* c/ Forcarei, 2.

◀ *Hostales* €30-70+: N-547: •*P* **Compás** *x11* © 981 511 309. •*Hs¨* **Platas** *x24* © 981 511 378. Adj. (rear) •*P.* **A Solaina** *x12* © 633 530 918 Rúa Picón, 3. •*P·* **Rosella** *x6* © 600 350 346. •*P·* **Una Estrella Dorada** *x4* © 630 018 363. *Av. de Santiago:* •*P* **9 de Abril** *x4* © 606 764 762. •*P·* **Pedrouzo** *x14* © 671 663 375 *www.pensionpedrouzo.com*. •*P* **Noja** *x12* © 627 127 696. •*P·* **Codesal** *x7* © 981 511 064 rua Codesal. •*Pr·* **Muiño** *x10* © 981 511 144. •*Pr·* **Maribel** *x5* © 609 459 966 adj. •*P* **Arca** *x7* © 657 888 594. •*P* **LO** *x12* © 981 510 401.

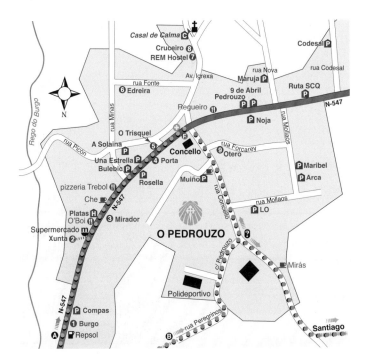

32 RIBADISO – PEDROUZO

‧‧‧‧‧‧‧‧‧‧	--- --- 12.9 --- ---	54%
▬▬▬	--- --- 8.4 --- ---	36%
▬▬▬	--- --- 2.4 --- ---	10%
Total km	**23.7 km** (*14.7 ml*)	

▲▲ Total ascent **1,150**m ± *2 hrs*
Alto ▲ Santa Irene **420**m (*1,378 ft*)
< Ⓐ Ⓗ > ⮕Arzúa **3.1 km** ⮕Salceda **14.1 km**
⮕Santa Irene **20.0 km** ⮕ A Rua **21.7 km**.

● **ARZUA: ❶** *Turismo* Praza do Peregrino ℃ 981 508 056. •*P*¨O Retiro *x18*
€30+ €48 ℃ 981 500 554. •*P* Puerta de Arzúa *x15* ℃ 9981 500 160. **Albergues**
Av. €12-15: ◀*Av. de Lugo* @Nº147 *Alb.* ❶ Los Tres Abetos *Priv.[42÷5]* ℃ 649
771 142 *www.tres-abetos.com* @Nº133 ❷ Selmo *Priv.[45÷1]* ℃ 981 939 018
www.oalberguedeselmo.com.@Nº132 •*H*¨Arzúa *x26* €60+ *www.hotelarzua.com*
@Nº107 ❸ Santiago Apóstol *Priv.[90÷4]* ℃ 981 508 132. @Nº133 ❹ Don
Quijote *Priv.**[48÷4] ℃ 981 500 139 ❺ Ultreia *Priv.**[28÷1] ℃ 981 500 471
❺ Albergue de Camino *Priv.[46÷4]*+ ℃ 981 500 415. ❼ Arzúa Turistico *Priv.*
[12÷2] +4 €45 ℃ 981 508 233 c/Rosalía de Castro, 2. ◀*rúa Cima do Lugar* =
Nº22 ❽ Cima do Lugar *Priv.[14÷1]* +8 €40+ ℃ 661 663 669. @Nº28 ❾ Cruce
De Caminos *Priv.[56÷8]* ℃ 881 817 716 *www.crucedecaminosarzua.com* @Nº7
❿ Casa del Peregrino *Priv.[14÷1]* ℃ 686 708 704 @Nº6 ⓫ Arzúa *Xunta [56÷3]*
€8 ℃ 660 396 824. ◀*Rua Carmen* @Nº7 ⓬San Francisco *Priv.[28÷2]* +2 €40 ℃
881 979 304 *www.alberguesanfrancisco.com* ⓭ Vía Láctea *Priv.[120÷12]* ℃ 981
500 581 *www.alberg{uevialactea.com* r/José Antonio. ⓮O Santo *Priv.[22÷1]* ℃
981 500 957 r/Xosé Neira Vilas, 4. ⓯ Peregrino *[20÷1]* ℃ 981 500 145 r/ Norte,
7. ⓰ Los Caminantes II *Priv.[28÷1]* ℃ 647 020 600 Av. de Santiago, 14. + 800m
⓱ A Conda *Priv.[18÷1]* +6 €45+ *www.pensionvilarino.com* c/Calexa, 92.

▮ **Taberna Velha:** ● (+500m) ●*Alb.* Camiño das Ocas *Priv.[30÷6]* €12 +4 €40
℃648 404 780 N-547 Burres. ●*Alb.* Taberna Velha *Priv.* [8÷1] €15 ℃ 687 543
810. ▮/¶ *bar TabernaNova* ▮**A Calle:** ●*Alb.* A Ponte de Ferreiros *Priv.[30÷2]*
€15 ℃ 665 641 877. ▮**Boavista:** ● (+500m) ●*Alb.* Turístico Salceda *Priv.[8÷1]*
€13 +15 €47 ℃ 981 502 767. ▮**Salceda:** •*P* Tasaga *x6* €50 ℃ 981 113 077. ●*Alb.*
Alborada *Priv.[10÷1]* €12 +4 €45 ℃ 620 151 209 •*P* Tía Teresa €45 ℃ 628
558 716 ▮**Brea:** •*P Mesón Brea* *x6* €30+ ℃ 981 511 040. •*H* O Pozo *x5* €50+.
●*Alb.* Andaina *Priv.[15].* ℃ 981 502 925 ▮**Santa Irene:** ●*Alb.* Santa Irene *Priv.**
[15÷2] €14 ℃ 981 511 000. ● (+700m) ●*Alb.* Rural Astar *Priv.[24÷2]* €14 ℃
981 511 463. ●*Alb.* Santa Irene *Xunta.[32÷2]* €8 N-547. ▮**A Rúa:** ●*Alb.* Espíritu
Xacobeo *[32÷2]* €12 +3 €60 ℃ 620 635 284 *www.espirituxacobeo.com.* •*H* O Pino
x15 ℃ 981 511 035. •*CR* O Acivro *x10* €75+ ℃ 981 511 316 + ▮↗. ▲Camping
Peregrino O Castiñeiro €12 ℃ 981 197 125 *www.campingperegrino.es.*

● *PEDROUZO p.93*

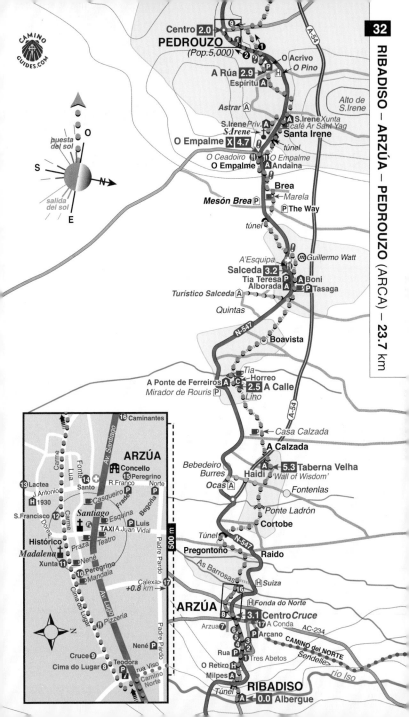

Centro **2.0**
PEDROUZO
(Pop.5,000)

O Acrivo
A Rúa 2.9 *O Pino* P H
Espíritu A

Astrar A

Alto de
S.Irene

S.Irene *Priv.* A S.Irene *Xunta*
S.Irene café Ar Sant Yag
S.Irene **Santa Irene**
O Empalme X 4.7
O Ceadoiro túnel
O Empalme O Empalme
A Andaina

Brea
Marela
Mesón Brea P P **The Way**

túnel

A'Esquipa m Guillermo Watt
Salceda 3.2
Tia Teresa P A **Boni**
Alborada A P P **Tasaga**
Turístico Salceda A

Quintas

Boavista

N-547

Tía
Horreo
A Ponte de Ferreiros A C **2.5 A Calle**
Mirador de Rouris P *Lino*

Casa Calzada

A Calzada
A **5.3 Taberna Velha**
Bebedeiro Haidi *'Wall of Wisdom'*
Burres
Ocas A *Fontenlas*

Ponte Ladrón
Cortobe

Túnel
Pregontoño **Raido**
As Barrosas
H *Suiza*

H *Fonda do Norte*
ARZÚA
3.1 Centro*Cruce*
Arzua 7 **17** A Conda AC-234
P **Arcano** CAMINO del NORTE
Rua P Sendelle
O Retiro H *Tres Abetos*
Milpes A *río Iso*
Túnel A **0.0 Albergue**
RIBADISO

ARZÚA (inset map)

16 Caminantes

ARZÚA
Concello
15 **Peregrino**
13 Lactea R.Franco Norte P
J.Antonio Santo
H 1930 Casqueiro
S.Francisco 12 *Santiago*
Histórico
Madalena
Xunta 11
10 **Peregrino**
Mandala
Calexa>
+0.8 km 17
Pizzeria
Nené P

Cruce 9
Cima do Lugar 8
Teodora
P
rua Viso
Camino
Norte

500 m
Padre Pardo

33 PEDROUZO (ARCA) – SANTIAGO

···········	--- --- 8.0 --- ---	40%
─────	--- --- 7.4 --- ---	38%
━━━━━	--- --- 4.4 --- ---	22%
Total km	**20.1** km	(*12.5 ml*)

Total ascent **720m** ± *1¼ hr*
Alto ▲ Monte do Gozo **370m** (*1,214 ft*)
< A H > ⮑ Amenal **3.4**km ⮑ Lavacolla **9.5**km
⮑ Monte Gozo **15.2** km ⮑ S. Lázaro **17.5** km

■ **Amenal:** •*H¨* Amenal *x13* €60+ ℭ 981 510 431. •*P.* Kilómetro 15 *x4* €50 ℭ 981 897 086. ■ **San Paio / Aeroporto:** ☕ *Casa Porta de Santiago* + •*P¨* The Last Twelve *x6* €60+ ℭ 619 904 743. •*H¨* Ruta Jacobea *x20* €90 ℭ 981 888 211. ■ **Lavacolla:** ☕/•*P* A Concha *x12* €30 ℭ 981 888 390. •*P* Dorotea *x18* €50 ℭ 619 424 969. •*P¨* San Paio *x45* €38-50 ℭ 981 888 205. •*P* Xacobeo *x4* €55 ℭ 608 363 658. ●*Alb.* Lavacolla *Priv.[32÷1]* €13 ℭ 981 897 274. •*H* *Garcas *x61* €35-50 ℭ 981 888 225 (+500m). ■ **Villamaior:** ☕/•Casa de Amancio ℭ 981 897 086 apartments €70+ ■ **San Marcos** ☕/▲ *San Marcos.* •*H¨* Akelarre *x12* €45 ℭ 981 552 689 *(+200m N-634).* ●*Alb.* Juan Pablo II *[68÷3]*+ €10 ℭ 981 597 222 (+350m).

■ **Monte del Gozo:** *Alb.*● Monte do Gozo *Xunta.[500÷120]* €8 +*100* €35 dbl. ℭ881 255 386 *www.montedogozo.com*

■ **Santiago de Compostela** *San Lazaro*: *Alb.*❶ San Lázaro *Xunta.[80÷6]* €10 ℭ981 571 488 adj. *Museo Pedagóxico.* •*H¨* San Jacobo *x20* €37+ ℭ 981 580 361 *www.hotelsanjacobo.com.* ❷ Dream in Santiago *Priv.[60÷6]* ℭ 981 943 208 *www.dreaminsantiago.com* ❸ Fin del Camino *Asoc.[112÷8]* €12 ℭ 981 587 324 (+*300m)* c/Moscova / r/Roma. ❹ A Fonte *Priv.[30÷1]* ℭ 881 290 468 *www.alberguesafonte.com* r/ Estocolmo 2. ❺ Santo Santiago *Priv.[40÷3]* €10-12 ℭ 657 402 403 r/ Valiño 3 adj. •*H* S.Lazaro *x31* €40+ ℭ 981 584 344. ❻ Monterey *Priv.[36÷3]* €15+ ℭ 655 484 299 r/ Fontiñas 65. ❼ La credencial *Priv.[36÷3]* €14+ ℭ 639 966 704 r/ Fonte Concheiros 13 (r/Altiboia). **Rúa da Fonte dos Concheiros:** ❽ SCQ *Priv.[24÷4]* €18+ ℭ 622 037 300. ❾Sixtos no Caminho *Priv.[40÷1]* €15-20 ℭ 881 024 195 *www.alberguesixtos.com* (corner of Av.Lugo) **Rúa dos Concheiros:** Nº48 ❿ Santos *Priv.[24÷3]* ℭ 881 169 386. Nº36 ⓫ La Estrella *Priv.[24÷1]* ℭ 881 973 926 *www.laestrelladesantiago.es* Nº10 ⓬ Porta Real *Priv.[20÷1]* ℭ 633 610 114 *www.albergueportareal.es.* ⓭ Seminario Menor *Conv.[170÷30]*€16 +*81* €22-44 ℭ 881 031 768 *www.alberguesdelcamino.com* Av. Quiroga Palacios Belvís **+500**m.

● **SANTIAGO de COMPOSTELA** *Centro p98.*

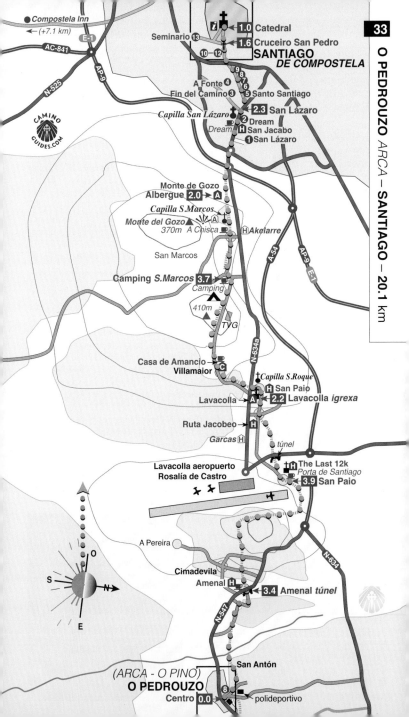

● Compostela Inn
← (+7.1 km)
E-1
AC-841
AP-9
N-525

CAMINO GUIDES.COM

Seminario 13

1.0 Catedral
1.6 Cruceiro San Pedro
SANTIAGO
DE COMPOSTELA

10 – 12

9
8
7
6

A Fonte 4
Fin del Camino 3
5 Santo Santiago

Capilla San Lázaro
2.3 San Lázaro
2 Dream
Dream San Jacabo
1 San Lázaro

Monte de Gozo
Albergue **2.0** → A

Capilla S.Marcos
Monte del Gozo ▲
370m *A Chisca* A
Akelarre

San Marcos

Camping *S.Marcos* 3.7
Camping ▲
410m ▲
TVG

Casa de Amancio
Villamaior C

†*Capilla S.Roque*
San Paio
Lavacolla → A **2.2** Lavacolla *igrexa*

Ruta Jacobeo → H
Garcas H
túnel

Lavacolla aeropuerto
Rosalía de Castro
✈
The Last 12k
Porta de Santiago
3.9 San Paio

A Pereira

Cimadevila
Amenal H **3.4** Amenal *túnel*

San Antón
N-547

(ARCA - O PINO)
O PEDROUZO
Centro **0.0** 8
polideportivo

O
S — N
E

● **Pilgrim's Reception Office** Rúa das Carretas, 33. ℭ 981 568 846 *(09:00-19.00)*
❶ **Turismo** *Centro*: r/ Vilar 63 ℭ 981 555 129 *May-Oct: 09:00-19.00 (winter 17:00)*
● **Laundromat:** 09:00-22:00 **SC18** Rúa San Clemente 18 ℭ 673 753 869.
● **Consignia Praca Quintana** (09:00-21:00) backpack storage €3 per day opp. Cath.
● **Intermodal Central Train/Bus Station** 700m (10 mins) South of Praza Galicia.

● *Albergues: €15-€25 (depending on season / beds per dormitory)* ❶–⓭ *see p.96*
⓮ **LoopINN** *(La Salle)* ℭ 981 585 667 c/ S.Clara. ⓯ **Meiga Backpackers** *Priv.*
[30÷5] ℭ 981 570 846 *www.meiga-backpackers.es* c/ Basquiños, 67. ❲**Centro
Histórico:** ⓰ Linares *[14÷2]* ℭ 981 943 253 r/ Algalia de Abaixo, 34. ⓱ **O Fogar
de Teodomiro** *Priv.[20÷5]*+ ℭ 981 582 920 Plaza de Algalia de Arriba 3. ⓲ **The
Last Stamp** *Priv.[62÷10]* ℭ 981 563 525 r/ Preguntorio 10. ⓳ **Azabache** *Priv.
[20÷5]* ℭ 981 071 254 c/Azabachería 15. ⓴ **Km.0** *Priv.[50÷10]* ℭ 881 974 992
www.santiagokm0.es r/ Carretas 11 (new renovation by pilgrim office) ㉑ **Blanco**
Priv.[20÷2]+4 €35-55 ℭ 881 976 850 r/ Galeras 30. ㉒ **Mundoalbergue** *Priv.
[34÷1]* ℭ 981 588 625 c/ San Clemente 26. ❲*Otros:* ㉓ **La Estación** *Priv.[24÷2]*
ℭ 981 594 624 r/ Xoana Nogueira 14 (adj. rail station +**2.9** km). ㉔ **Compostela
Inn** *Priv.[120÷30]*+ ℭ 981 819 030 off *AC-841 (+6.0 km).*

● *Hoteles €30–60:* •*Hs* **Moure** ℭ 981 583 637 r/dos Loureiros. •*H* **Fonte S.
Roque** ℭ 981 554 447 r/do Hospitallilo 8. •*Hs* **Estrela** ℭ 981 576 924 Plaza
de San Martín Pinario 5. •*Hs* **San Martín Pinario** *x127* ℭ 981 560 282 *www.
hsanmartinpinario.com* Praza da Inmaculada. •**Pico Sacro** r/San Francisco 22 ℭ
981 584 466. •*H*¨ **Montes** ℭ 981 574 458 *www.hotelmontes.es* r/ Raíña 11. **Rúa
Fonseca Nº1** •*P* **Fonseca** ℭ 603 259 337. **Nº5** •*Hs* **Libredon** 981 576 520 & •*P*
Barbantes /**Celsa** ℭ981 583 271 on r/ Franco 3. **Rúa Vilar Nº8** •*H*¨ **Rua Villar** ℭ
981 519 858. **Nº17** •*H*¨ **Airas Nunes** ℭ 981 569 350. **Nº65** •*Hs*¨ **Suso** ℭ 981 586
611 *www.hostalsuso.com*. **Nº76** •*Hs* **Santo Grial** ℭ 629 515 961. •**Anosa Casa** ℭ
981 585 926 r/ Entremuralles 9 adj. •*Hs* **Mapoula** ℭ 981 580 124. •*Hs* **Alameda**
ℭ 981 588 100 San Clemente 32. ❲*€60–90:* •*H* **A Casa Peregrino** ℭ 981 573 931
c/ Azabachería. •**Entrecercas** ℭ 981 571 151 r/Entrecercas. **Porta de Pena Nº17**
•*H* **Costa Vella** ℭ 981 569 530 (+ Jardín) **Nº5** •*P* **Casa Felisa** ℭ 981 582 602
(+Jardín). •**MV Algalia** ℭ 981 558 111 Praza Algalia de Arriba 5. •*H*¨ **Pazo De
Altamira** ℭ 981 558 542 r/ Altamira, 18. ❲*€100+* •*H*¨¨ **San Francisco** Campillo
de San Francisco ℭ 981 581 634. •*H*¨¨ **Hostal de los Reyes Católicos** (**Parador**)
Plaza Obradoiro ℭ 981 582 200.

Centro Histórico: ❶ Convento de Santo
Domingo de Bonaval XIIIth *(panteón de
Castelao, Rosalía de Castro y museo do Pobo
Galego).* ❷ Mosteiro de San Martín Pinario
XVIth *y museo* ❸ Pazo de Xelmirez XIIth
❹ Catedral XIIth –XVIIIth *Portica de Gloria,
claustro, museo e tesouro* ❺ Hostal dos Reis
Católicos XVth *Parador* ❻ Pazo de Raxoi
XVIIIth *Presendencia da Xunta* ❼ Colexio
de Fonseca XVIth *universidade y claustro*
❽ Capela y Fonte de Santiago ❾ Casa do
Deán XVIIIth *Oficina do Peregrino (original).*
❿ Casa Canónica *museo Peregrinaciónes.*
⓫ Mosteiro de San Paio de Antealtares XVth
Museo de Arte Sacra. ⓬ S.Maria Salomé XIIth.

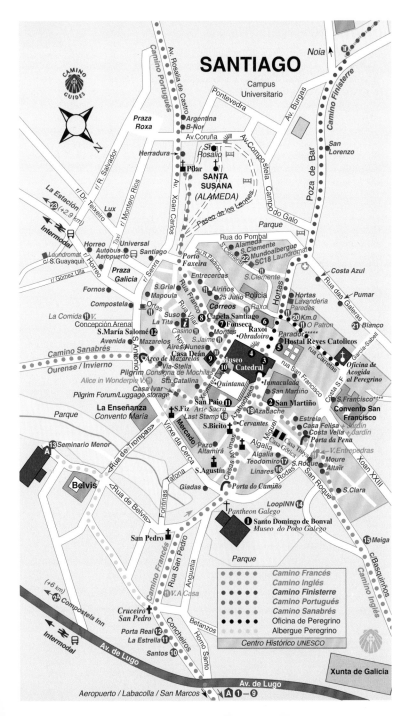

Claves para las leyendas del mapa:

Total km	Distancia total de la etapa indicada
	Adaptado para el desnivel (100 m verticales + 10 minutos)
_(850m)_ **Alto** ▲	Curva de desnivel / Punto más elevado de cada etapa
< 🏠 🏥 >	Alojamiento intermedio
◄ **3.5**	Distancia exacta entre puntos (3,5 km = ± 1 hora de camino)
→ 50m > / ^ / <	Distancias parciales: a150 m a la derecha>/seguir recto^/<izquierda
	c. = aprox. / adj. = junto / incl. = incluido
....	Camino o sendero (_verde_: caminos naturales / _gris_: hormigón)
──○──	Carretera secundaria (_gris_: asfalto) / Rotonda
══N-11══	Carretera principal [N-] (_rojo_: mayor tráfico y peligro)
══A-1══	Autopista (_azul_: color habitual)
+++++++●	Vía de tren / Estación
●●●●●●	El camino primordial de peregrinación: el camino interior del Alma.
●●●●●●	Ruta principal (_amarillo_: ± 80% peregrinos)
●●●●●●	Ruta escénica (_verde_: más alejada / menos servicios)
●●●●●●	Rodeo opcional a un punto de interés (_turquesa_)
●●●●●●	Ruta por carretera (_gris_: más asfalto)
⊠ ❓ ⦸	Cruce / Punto de Opción / Atención especial
⊼ ⋎ †	Molino de viento / Mirador / Antena de radio
▪▬▪/▪▬▪	Frontera estatal / Límites de provinciales
～/～	Río / Arroyo
◯/◯	Lago o estuario / Bosque
ⵜ ⵌ †	Iglesia / Capilla / Crucero
ⓕ ☕ ⦙	Fuente de agua potable [♨] / Café bar ☕ / Mini-mercado 🛒
¶ _menú_ _V._	Restaurante / Menú del peregrino / _V._ Vegetariano
🛈 🏨 ✗	Turismo / Quinta o Pazo / Área de descanso
✚ ✛ ✉	Farmacia / Hospital / Correos
✈ 🚌 ⛽	Aeropuerto / Estación de autobuses / Gasolinera
⁘ XII	Monumento histórico / Siglo XII
Ⓐ❶ **ⒶⒶ**	Albergue(s) de peregrinos / ●_Alb._ Albergue Cerrado
Ⓗ Ⓟ Ⓒ	Hotel _H°–H****_ 30–90 / Pensión _P*_ €20+ / Casa rural _CR_ €35+
Ⓠ **B.V.**	_Quinta Q_ €50–90 / Estación de bomberos _BV_ € 5–10
Ⓗ Ⓐ Ⓙ	_(Alojamiento fuera de ruta)_
_[32]_	Número de plazas de cama (normalmente literas)
_[÷4]+_	÷ número de dormitorios + _también habitaciones privadas_
Par.	Albergue parroquial _donación_ €5+
Conv.	Albergue en un convento o monasterio _donación_ €5+
Muni.	Albergue municipal €5+
Xunta	Albergue de la Xunta de Galicia €6
Asoc.	Albergue de una asociación
Priv. (*)	Albergue privado €10–15
	*_Los precios medios (temporada baja) para efectos comparativos_
	Hs.=Hostal / Hr.=Hotel Residencial
▭	Plano de ciudad
(Pop.–Alt. m)	Población – Altitud en metro
▭	Periferia (gris)
▭	Centro Histórico (marrón)

Introducción: En las vidas de todos nosotros hay un exceso de parafernalia. Con la pretensión de aligerar la carga, hemos creado esta delgada edición de mapas. Ello ha sido posible gracias al trabajo desinteresado de las asociaciones de peregrinos que han señalizado el recorrido de tal forma que, hoy en día, tan solo necesitamos la información más básica para alcanzar nuestro destino. Resulta difícil perderse si en todo momento permanecemos concentrados y atentos a las flechas amarillas que apuntan en dirección a Santiago: en la concentración está la clave. Tómate un tiempo para familiarizarte con los símbolos del mapa que hallarás en la página de enfrente.

El estándar y el costo de alojamiento peregrino varía de los albergues municipales que ofrece servicios básicos de € 5 (sin reserva previa) a los albergues privados a partir de € 10 + pero a menudo con servicios adicionales tales como lavadoras y secadoras. Un menú peregrino comprende una comida básica de 3 platos con vino a un costo de alrededor de 9 €.

Estos mapas multilingües son un reconocimiento al compañerismo internacional del camino. Éste favorece el sentimiento de camaradería y comunión; una intención espiritual compartida que yace en el corazón de la peregrinación. Es esta focalización transcendente lo que distingue al peregrinaje del senderismo de larga distancia. Te recomendamos usar una guía con notas sobre cómo preparar bien un viaje largo de esta naturaleza, como el libro complementario *A Pilgrim's Guide to the Camino Francés*, un manual práctico y místico para el peregrino moderno *(Inglés)*.

Todos recorremos dos caminos simultáneamente: el camino exterior, por el que arrastramos nuestro cuerpo, y el camino interior del alma. Debemos ser conscientes de los dos y tomarnos el tiempo para prepararnos adecuadamente. El camino tradicional del peregrino es viajar solo, a pie, cargando con todas las posesiones materiales que podamos necesitar en el viaje que tenemos por delante. Esto brinda la primera lección al peregrino: dejar atrás todo lo superfluo y viajar tan sólo con lo estrictamente necesario. La preparación para el camino interior es similar: comenzamos soltando la basura psíquica acumulada a lo largo de los años, como resentimientos, prejuicios y sistemas de creencias pasados de moda. Con una mente y un corazón abiertos asimilaremos con mayor facilidad las lecciones con las que nos encontraremos a lo largo de este Camino de las Averiguaciones.

Llevamos mucho tiempo dormidos. Pese al caótico mundo que nos rodea, o tal vez a causa de él, hay algo que nos sacude para que despertemos de nuestra amnesia colectiva. Una señal de este despertar es el número de personas que se sienten atraídas por hacer los caminos. El ritmo frenético de la vida moderna, que experimentamos no sólo en el trabajo sino también en nuestra vida familiar y en la social, hace que cada vez revoloteamos más lejos de nuestro centro. Hemos consentido en ser arrojados a la superficie de nuestras vidas, al confundir estar ocupados con estar vivos, pero esta existencia superficial resulta intrínsecamente insatisfactoria.

La peregrinación nos brinda la oportunidad de reducir el ritmo y de dotar a nuestras vidas de una cierta amplitud. En este espacio más tranquilo se puede reflexionar acerca del significado más profundo de nuestras vidas y las razones por las que hemos venido aquí. El camino nos anima a hacernos la pregunta perenne: ¿quién soy? Y, lo que resulta crucial, nos proporciona el tiempo para poder comprender y asimilar las respuestas. Así que no te apresures en recorrer el camino: tómate el tiempo que sea necesario, porque podría resultar ser el punto de inflexión de tu vida.

Buen camino.

Zeichenerklärung:

Total km Gesamtentfernung für angezeigte Etappe

An Höhenunterschied angepasst (100 m Höhe + 10 minuten)

(850m) **Alto** ▲ Etappenprofil / Höchster Punkt jeder Etappe

< Ⓐ Ⓗ > Unterkunft unterwegs

◀ **3.5** Genaue Entfernung zwischen Punkten (3,5 km = ± 1 Stunde Wandern)

→● 50m > / ^ / < Zwischenentfernungen – in 150 m nach rechts>/geradeaus^/<links

c. = (Ungefähr) / adj. = Angrenzend / incl. = Inklusive <nach links

Weg oder Pfad (*grün*: natürliche Wege / *grau*: beton)

Nebenstraße (*grau*: Asphalt) / Kreisverkehr

N-11 Hauptstraße [N-] (*rot*: mehr Verkehr und größere Gefahr)

A-1 Autobahn (*blau*: herkömmliche Farbe)

++++++● Bahn / Bahnhof

●●●●●● Der ursprüngliche pfad ist der innere Pfad der Seele

●●●●●● Hauptroute (*gelb*: ± 80% pilger / vorwiegend Wege)

●●●●●● Route mit Ausblick (*grün*: abgelegener / weniger Versorgung)

●●●●●● Möglicher Abstecher desvío zu Sehenswürdigkeit (*türkis*)

●●●●●● Landstraßen-Route (*grau*: mehr Asphalt)

Ⓧ ❓ ❶ Kreuzung *cruce* / Optionspunkt / Besondere Vorsicht

⋏ ⿻ ⼓ Windrad / Aussichtspunkt / Antennenmast

▪–▪–/▪ Landesgrenze / Provinzgrenze

〜/〜 Fluss *río* / Bach

◯/⬭ See oder Flussmündung / Wald

✝ ⼓ † Kirche / Kapelle / Kreuz am Wegesrand

Ⓕ 🍽 ⾳ Trinkwasser-Quelle *fuente* [☕] / Café Bar 🍴/ Mini-Markt 🛒

🍴 *menú V.* Restaurant / Pilgermenü *menú* / Vegetarier

ⓘ 🏯 ✕ Tourismus / Herrenhaus / Rastplatz *Área de descanso*

➕ ➕ ✉ Apotheke *farmacia* / Krankenhaus / Post *correos*

⊕ 🚌 ⛽ Flughafen / Busbahnhof / Tankstelle

⁚⁚ XII Altes Denkmal / 12. Jahrhundert

Ⓐ❶ Ⓐ Ⓐ Pilgerherberge(n) *Albergue(s)* / ●*Alb.* Albergue geschlossen

Ⓗ Ⓟ Ⓒ Hotel *H˙–H˙˙˙˙* 30–90 / Pension *P˙* €20+ / *Casa rural CR* €35+

Ⓠ B.V. Herrenhaus *Quinta Q* €50–90 / Feuerwehrhaus *Bombeiros BV* €5–10

Ⓗ Ⓐ Ⓙ *(Unterkunft abseits der Route)*

[32] Anzahl der Bettplätze (gewöhnlich Etagenbetten *literas*)

[÷4]+ ÷ Anzahl der Schlafsäle + *auch Privatzimmer*

Par. Gemeinde-Herberge (Kirchengemeinde) Spende *donación* (€5+)

Conv. Klosterherberge Spende *donación* (€5+)

Muni. Städtische Herberge €5+

Xunta Herberge der Landesregierung Galiziens (Xunta) €6

Asoc. Herberge einer Vereinigung €5–8

Priv. (*) Private Herberge €10–15

˙*Alle Preise sind annähernd und nur zum Vergleich angegeben*
Hs.=Hostal / Hr.=Hotel Residencial

Stadtplan

(Pop.–Alt. m) Stadtbevölkerung – Höhe in Metern

Außenbezirke (*grau*)

Altstadt centro histórico (*braun*)

Einführung: Wir alle haben zu viel Trödel in unserem Leben – um die Last zu erleichtern, haben wir diese schlanke Karten-Edition hergestellt. Ermöglicht wurde dies durch die selbstlose Arbeit von Pilgerorganisationen, die die Route dergestalt markiert haben, dass wir heute nur die grundlegendste Information brauchen, um an unser Ziel zu gelangen. Es ist schwer, sich zu verlaufen; wir müssen nur in jedem Moment gegenwärtig sein und auf die gelben Pfeile achten, die den Weg nach Santiago weisen – Achtsamkeit ist der Schlüssel. Nimm dir Zeit, dich mit den Karten-Symbolen auf der gegenüberliegenden Seite vertraut zu machen.

Der Standard und die Kosten der Pilger Unterkunft variiert von *Xunta* Hostels bieten grundlegende Einrichtungen ab € 5 (kein Vorreservierung) an private Hostels ab € 10 +, aber oft mit zusätzlichen Einrichtungen wie Waschmaschinen und Trockner. Eine grundlegende 3-Gänge-Menü mit Wein *(menú peregrino)* kostet ca. € 9.

Die mehrsprachigen Karten würdigen die internationale Gemeinschaft des Camino. Dieser för¬dert das Gefühl von Freundschaft und Vereinigung; ein ge¬meinsames geistiges Ansinnen, das im Herzen der Wallfahrt liegt. Es ist dieser Fokus auf das Transzendente, was eine Wallfahrt vom Fernwandern unter¬scheidet.

Wir alle reisen gleichzeitig auf zwei Wegen; der äußere, entlang dessen wir unseren Körper schleppen, und der innere Weg der Seele. Wir müssen uns beider bewusst sein und uns die Zeit nehmen für eine entsprechende Vorbereitung. Traditionsgemäß ist der Weg des Wallfahrers eine Reise zu Fuß, alleine; wir tragen allen materiellen Besitz, den wir für die bevorstehende Fahrt benötigen mögen, mit uns. Dies bringt auch die erste Lektion für den Pilger – alles Überflüssige hinter sich zu lassen und nur mit dem wahrhaft Notwendigen zu reisen. Die Vorbereitung für den inneren Weg ist ähnlich – sie beginnt mit dem Ablegen vom psychischen Müll, der sich über die Jahre angehäuft hat, wie Groll, Vorurteile und überholte Glaubenssysteme. Mit offenem Verstand und offenem Herzen werden wir umso leichter die Lehren aufnehmen, die entlang dieses uralten Weges der Suche gefunden werden können.

Wir haben lange geschlafen. Trotz der chaotischen Welt um uns herum, oder vielleicht gerade ihretwegen, schüttelt uns etwas, auf dass wir aus unserer kollektiven Amnesie erwachen. Ein Zeichen dieses Erwachens ist die Anzahl der Menschen, die sich angezogen fühlen, die Caminos zu erwandern. Das hektische Tempo des modernen Lebens, das wir nicht nur in unserer Arbeit, sondern auch in unserem familiären und gesellschaftlichen Leben erfahren, wirbelt uns immer weiter nach außen, weg von unserem Zentrum. Wir haben es zugelassen, an die Oberfläche unseres Lebens geworfen zu werden – wir verwechseln Geschäftigkeit mit Lebendigkeit, doch dieses oberflächliche Dasein ist in sich unbefriedigend.

Eine Wallfahrt bietet uns die Gelegenheit, langsamer zu werden und etwas Weite in unser Leben hineinzulassen. In diesem stilleren Umfeld können wir über die tiefere Bedeutung unseres Lebens nachdenken und über den Grund, wozu wir hierher kamen. Der Camino ermutigt uns, die immerwährende Frage zu stellen – wer bin ich? Und entscheidend ist: er bietet uns Zeit dafür, die Antworten zu verstehen und zu integrieren. Also hetzt nicht auf dem Camino – nimm dir die Zeit, die er erfordert, denn er könnte sich als ein entscheidender Wendepunkt in deinem Leben entpuppen.

Buen camino.

Legenda:

Total km   Distanza totale della tappa indicata

Adatto al dislivello (100 m verticali + 10 minuto)

(850m) **Alto** ▲   Curva di dislivello / Punto più elevato di ogni tappa

< 🅰 🅷 >   Alloggio intermedio *(di solito meno occupato)*

◄ **3.5**   Distanza esatta tra punti (3,5 km = ± 1'ora di cammino)

●— 50 m > / ^ / <   Distanze parziali: a 150 m a destra > / proseguire dritto ^ / < a sinistra
     c.= circa / adj.= adiacente / incl.= incluso

::::::::::::::   Cammino o sentiero (*verde*: cammini naturali / pista di ghiaia)

—○—   Strada secondaria (*grigio*: asfalto) / Rotonda

N-11   Strada principale [N-] (*rosso*: maggiore traffico e pericolo)

A-1   Autostrada (*azzurra*: colore abituale)

+++++++●   Via di treno / Stazione

● ● ● ● ● ●   Percorso principale del pellegrinaggio; il percorso interno dell'Anima.

● ● ● ● ● ●   Itinerario consigliato (*giallo*: ± 80% dei pellegrini / cammini naturali)

● ● ● ● ● ●   Itinerario scenico (*verde*: più lontana / meno servizi)

● ● ● ● ● ●   Giro opzionale a un punto di interesse (*azzurrino*)

● ● ● ● ● ●   Itinerario per strada (*grigio*: più asfalto)

🆇   ❓   🛇   Croce / Punto di Opzione / Attenzione speciale

ↂ   ⅄   ↑   Mulino di vento / Belvedere / Antenna di radio

·—·/·—·   Frontiera statale / Limiti di provinciali

∼ / ⌒   Fiume / Fiumicello

◯ / ◯   Lago oppure estuario / Bosco

⛪   ⛪   ✝   Chiesa / Cappella / Croce

🅖   🍺   🛒   Fontana di acqua potabile *Fuente* [⛲] / Caffè bar 🍺 / Mini-mercato 🛒

🍴 *menú*   *V.*   Ristorante / menú de peregrino / vegetariano

🅘   🏠   ✖   Turismo / casa signorile / Picnic

➕   ➕   ✉   Farmacia / Ospedale / Posta

⊕   🚌   ⛽   Aeroporto / Stazione degli autobus / Distributore di benzina

⁛   XII   Monumento storico / Secolo XII

🅐❶   🅐 🅐   Ostello (-i) di pellegrino *Alb.* / ●*Alb.* Ostello chiuso

🅗   🅟   🅒   Hotels *H-H*¨¨¨¨€30-90 / Pensione *P*˙€20+ / Casa rurale *CR* €35+

🅠   B.V.   Casa signorile *Quinta Q* €50-90 / Stazione di pompieri *B.V.* €5-10

🅗   🅐   🅙   *Alloggio fuori itinerario*

   [32]   Numero di posti letto (in genere letti a castello)

   [÷4]+   ÷ numero di dormitori + anche stanze private €20+

   Par.   Ostello parrocchiale donazione (€5+)

   Conv.   Ostello in un convento o monastero donazione (€5+)

   Muni.   Ostello municipale €5+

   Xunta   Ostello della Xunta di Galizia €6

   Asoc.   Ostello di un'associazione

   Priv. (*)   Ostello privato (della Red di Albergues* Rete di Ostelli) €10–15
     I prezzi sono indicativi; ai soli fini comparativi
     Hs.=Hostal / Hr.=Hostal Residenziali

▢   Cartina della città

(Pop.–Alt. m)   Popolazione – Altitudine in metri

▢   Periferia (*grigio*)

▢   Centro Storico (*marrone*)

Introduzione: Nelle vite di tutti noi c'è un eccesso di accessori. Per cercare di alleggerire il carico, abbiamo creato questa edizione di mappe ,leggera'. Questo è stato possibile grazie al lavoro disinteressato delle Associazioni di Pellegrini che hanno segnato il percorso, il che fa sì che oggi ci bastino poche informazioni di base per raggiungere la destinazione. È difficile perdersi se si rimane costantemente concentrati e attenti alle frecce gialle che puntano verso Santiago: la chiave è l'attenzione. Prendi il tempo necessario per familiarizzarti con i simboli della mappa che trovi nella pagina di fronte.

Il comfort e il costo degli alloggi per i pellegrini varia dagli ostelli parrocchiali, che chiedono una libera offerta, a quelli municipali, che offrono servizi di base a partire da €5 (senza obbligo di prenotazione), agli ostelli privati che vanno dai €10 in su, ma che spesso offrono servizi aggiuntivi come lavatrice e asciugatrice, quest'ultima una gran comodità nei giorni di pioggia. Un pasto base di 3 portate con vino (menú peregrino) costa circa €9.

Queste cartine multilingue sono un riconoscimento alla fratellanza internazionale del Cammino. Questa favorisce il sentimento di cameratismo e comunione: un'intenzione spirituale condivisa che costituisce il cuore del pellegrinaggio. È questo che distingue il pellegrinaggio dal trekking di lunga distanza.

Tutti percorriamo simultaneamente due cammini: il cammino esteriore, che percorriamo fisicamente, e quello interiore dell'anima. Dobbiamo affrontare tutti e due con consapevolezza, e prenderci il tempo necessario per prepararci adeguatamente. Tradizionalmente il pellegrino viaggia da solo, a piedi, portandosi dietro tutto ciò di cui ha bisogno per il viaggio. In questo modo il pellegrino impara la prima lezione: lasciare indietro tutto il superfluo e viaggiare solo con quanto strettamente necessario. La preparazione per il cammino interiore è simile: si comincia buttando via la spazzatura psichica accumulata lungo gli anni, come risentimenti, pregiudizi e sistemi di credenze obsoleti. Con una mente e un cuore aperti si assimilano più facilmente le lezioni che si imparano lungo questo antico Cammino di Ricerca.

È da tanto tempo che siamo addormentati. Malgrado il mondo caotico che ci gira attorno, o forse proprio grazie ad esso, sentiamo qualcosa che ci spinge a svegliarci dalla nostra amnesia collettiva. Un segnale di questo risveglio è il numero di persone che si sentono attratte dai pellegrinaggi. Il ritmo frenetico della vita moderna, non solo al lavorativa ma anche famigliare e sociale, ci spinge sempre più lontano dal nostro centro. Ci lasciamo trascinare sempre più verso aspetti superficiali delle nostre vite, confondendo l'essere occupati con l'essere vivi, ma questa esistenza superficiale risulta sostanzialmente insoddisfacente.

Il pellegrinaggio ci offre l'occasione di rallentare il ritmo e di dare un po' di respiro alla nostra vita. In questo spazio più tranquillo possiamo riflettere sul significato profondo della vita e sulle ragioni per cui siamo venuti qui. Il Cammino ci spinge a farci l'eterna domanda: chi sono io? E, cosa più importante, ci da il tempo di poter capire e assimilare le risposte. Quindi non percorrere il Cammino di fretta: prendi il tempo di cui hai bisogno, perché potrebbe diventare un punto di svolta della tua vita.

Buen camino.

Légende:

Total km	Distance totale de l'étape
	Distance équivalente avec ajout de la déclivité (100 m vertical
(850m)**Alto**▲	Courbes de niveau / Point culminant de l'étape +10 minutes)
< Ⓐ Ⓗ >	Hébergement en cours d'étape
◀ **3.5**	Distance précise entre points (3,5 km = ± 1 heure de marche)
–●150m > / ^ / <	Distances intermédiaires : à 150m tourner à droite> / ^tout droit /
	à gauche>
.... /	Sentier ou piste (*vert* : en terre / *gris*: béton)
══○══	Route secondaire (*gris*: asphalte) / Rond-point
══N-11══	Route principale [N]-(*rouge* : circulation plus importante et danger)
══A-1══	Autoroute (*bleu*: couleur conventionnelle)
+++++++++●	Voie ferrée / Gare
X **?** **0**	Carrefour / Point de l'option / Faire particulièrement attention
● ● ● ● ●	Route principale (*jaune*: ± 80% des pèlerins)
● ● ● ● ●	Itinéraire par la route (*gris* : plus d'asphalte)
● ● ● ● ●	Route panoramique (*vert*: moins de services / plus à l'écart)
● ● ● ● ●	Détour facultatif vers un point d'intérêt (*turquoise*)
↑ ☀ ⊺	Moulin à vent / Point de vue / Antenne radio
▪—▪—▪/▪▪▪	Frontière nationale / limite de province
∿ / ∿	Rivière / Ruisseau
⬭ / ⬭	Lac ou estuaire / Forêt
✝ ⚲ †	Église / Chapelle / Croix
ⓕ 🍺 🏪	Fontaine d'eau potable [♨] / Café-bar 🍴 / Supérette 🛒
¶ *menú V.*	restaurant / avec menu du pèlerin / Végétarien
🛈 🏠 ✗	Tourisme / Quinta ou manoir / table de pique-nique
➕ ✚ ✉	Pharmacie / Hôpital / Poste
✈ 🚌 ⛽	Aéroport / Gare routière / Station Service
⚫⚫ XIIth c	Site historique / XIIe siècle
Ⓐ❶ Ⓐ Ⓐ	Auberge(s) de pèlerins / ●A*lb.* Auberge fermé / *CR* Incl. 35 € +
Ⓗ Ⓟ Ⓒ	Hôtel *H* –*H*¨¨¨¨ 30–90 € / Pension *P* 20 €+ / Chambre d'hôte
Ⓗ Ⓐ Ⓙ	*Hébergement hors itinéraire*
[32]	Nombre de places-lits (en général superposés)
[÷4]+	÷ nombre de dortoirs + *aussi des chambres privées*
Par.	Auberge de paroisse (don / 5 €)
Conv.	Auberge dans un couvent ou monastère (don / 5 € +)
Muni.	Auberge municipale 5 €
Xunta	Auberge du gouvernement *Xunta de Galicia* € 6
Asoc.	Auberge d'association € 7 / Incl. petit déjeuner compris
Priv. (*)	Auberge privée (réseau des auberges*) 10 € + / Incl.
	Tous les prix sont approximatifs; à des fins de comparaison
▭	Plan de ville
(Pop.–Alt. m)	Population - Altitude en mètres
▭	Banlieue (gris)
▭	Centre historique centro histórico (brun)

Introduction : Dans la vie de chacun de nous, il y a trop d'objets matériels. Dans le but d'alléger cette charge, nous avons créé une édition légère de cartes. Cela a été possible grâce au travail désintéressé des associations de pèlerins qui ont si bien marqué le parcours qu'aujourd'hui, pour atteindre la destination, on a simplement besoin de renseignements de base. Il est difficile de se perdre si on reste à tout moment concentré et attentif aux flèches jaunes indiquant Santiago : la clé, c'est la concentration. Prenez le temps de vous familiariser avec les symboles sur la page opposée.

La norme et le coût de l'hébergement pèlerin varie d'auberges *municipal* offrant des installations de base de 5 € (pas de réservation) à auberges privées à partir de € 10 + mais souvent avec des équipements supplémentaires tels que machines à laver et sécher. Une base repas de 3 plats avec du vin (Menú peregrino) coûte environ € 9

Ces cartes multilingues témoignent de la solidarité internationale du *Camino* qui favorise un sentiment de camaraderie et de fraternité, et d'une démarche spirituelle partagée qui est au cœur du pèlerinage. C'est ce qui distingue le pèlerinage de la grande randonnée.

Nous avançons tous en même temps sur deux voies : la voie externe, pour laquelle nous entrainons notre corps, et la voie interne qui correspond au voyage intérieur de l'âme. Nous devons être conscients de ces deux voies et prendre le temps de bien nous préparer. La tradition veut que le pèlerin chemine tout seul, à pied, portant ce qui lui est nécessaire pour le voyage. C'est la première leçon du pèlerin : laisser derrière soi tout le superflu et voyager avec seulement ce qui est nécessaire. La préparation pour le chemin interne est similaire : nous commençons par nous débarrasser des scories psychiques accumulées au fil des ans, comme les ressentiments, les préjugés et les systèmes de croyance dépassés. Avec un esprit et un cœur plus ouverts, on peut plus facilement assimiler les leçons que l'on tire le long de cette très ancienne voie de découverte.

Longtemps nous sommes restés endormis. Malgré le monde chaotique qui nous entoure, ou peut-être à cause de lui, il y a quelque chose qui nous travaille, et nous nous réveillons alors de notre amnésie collective. Un signe de cet éveil est le nombre de personnes qui sont attirées par les pèlerinages. Le rythme effréné de la vie moderne dont nous faisons l'expérience non seulement au travail, mais aussi dans notre vie familiale et sociale, nous propulse plus loin de notre centre. Nous nous sommes laissés projeter sur la surface de nos vies, en confondant celle-ci avec l'hyperactivité, mais cette existence superficielle n'est pas intrinsèquement satisfaisante.

Le pèlerinage nous donne l'occasion de ralentir le rythme et de donner une respiration à nos vies. Dans cet espace silencieux, on peut réfléchir sur le sens profond de notre existence et sur les raisons de notre présence sur terre. Le *Camino* nous incite à nous poser l'éternelle question : qui suis-je ? Et il nous donne le temps – ce qui est crucial – de comprendre et d'assimiler les réponses. Alors ne vous précipitez pas pour parcourir la route : prenez le temps nécessaire, car c'est peut-être le tournant de votre vie. Quelle que soit la voie que vous choisissez, votre destination finale est la même. Le seul choix que vous ayez est le temps que vous prenez pour l'atteindre.

Buen camino.

Explicação das legendas dos mapas:

Total km	Distância total da etapa
	Ajustado para subida (100 m na vertical + 10 minutos)
(850m) **Alto** ▲	Linha de relevo / Ponto mais alto da etapa
< Ⓐ Ⓗ >	Alojamento intermédio
◄ **3.5**	Distância exacta entre pontos (3.5 km = ± 1 hora andar)
● 50m > / ^ / <	Distâncias intermédias 150 metros virar à direita> / seguir em frente^...
	c. = (cerca de) / adj. = adjacente / incl. = Incluindo
....	Caminho ou carreiro (*verde*: caminho rural / *cinzento*: concreto)
━○━	Estrada secundária (*cinzento*: asfalto) / Rotunda
N-11	Estrada principal (*vermelho*: mais trânsito e perigo)
A-1	Auto-estrada (*azul*: cor convencional das auto-estradas)
++++++●	Estação caminho-de-ferro
●●●●●●	O caminho primordial de peregrinação: o caminho interior da Alma
●●●●●●	Percurso principal (*amarelo*: ± 80% de todos os peregrinos)
●●●●●●	Percurso rural alternativo (*verde*: mais afastado/menos pontos de apoio)
●●●●●●	Desvio opcional para ponto de interesse (*turquesa*)
●●●●●●	Percurso alternativo (*cinzento*: mais estradas – asfalto)
⊠ ⁇ ⓪	Cruzamento / Opção / ¡Cuidado!
↑ ⩊ ╎	Moinho / Miradouro / Antena de transmissão
·—·/·—·	Fronteira nacional / Limite de província
～ / ～	Rio / Ribeiro
◯ / ◯	Estuário marítimo ou fluvial / Área florestal
✝ ✝ ✝	Igreja / Capela / Cruzeiro
Ⓖ 🍺 🛒	Fonte [♨] / Café-bar 🍺 / Mini-mercado 🛒
🍴 *menú V.*	Restaurante / menu peregrino / vegetariana
ℹ 🏠 ✕	Posto de turismo / Solar / Picnic
✚ ✚ ✉	Farmácia / Hospital / Posto de correios
✈ 🚌 ⛽	Aeroporto / Estação autocarros / Bomba gasolina
⚫⚫ XII	Monumento histórico / Século 12
Ⓐ❶ Ⓐ Ⓐ	Albergue(s) de peregrinos *Alb.* / ●A*lb.* Albergue fechado
Ⓗ Ⓟ Ⓒ	Hotel *H* –*H*"" €30–90 / Pensão *P* €20+ / Casa rural *CR* €35+
Ⓠ B.V.	Quinta *Q* €50–90 / Quartel de Bombeiros *BV* € 5–10
Ⓗ Ⓐ Ⓙ	*(alojamento perto mas fora)*
[32]	Número de lugares (geralmente beliches)
[÷4]+	÷ numero de dormitórios + *quartos particulares*
Par.	Alojamento paroquial (da igreja) *donativo* €5+
Conv.	Alojamento em convento ou mosteiro *donativo* €5+
Muni.	Alojamento municipal €5+
Xunta	Alojamento oficial *Xunta Galego* €6
Asoc.	Alojamento de uma associação €7+
Priv. (*)	Alojamento privado €10–15
	Os preços são aproximados e apenas a título de comparação *Hs.=Hostal / Hr.=Hotel Residencial*
▭	Planta da cidade
(Pop.–Alt. m)	População - altitude, em metros
▭	Subúrbios (*cinzento*)
▭	Centro histórico (*castanho*)

Introdução: Todos carregamos demasiados acessórios nas nossas vidas – num esforço para aliviar o peso produzimos este leve e fino volume de mapas básicos. Isto foi possível devido ao trabalho altruísta de organizações de apoio aos peregrinos que sinalizaram o Caminho de modo a que, hoje em dia, necessitemos de um mínimo de informações para nos levar ao destino. Será difícil perdermo-nos se nos mantivermos atentos às setas amarelas que indicam o caminho até Santiago.

O padrão e custo de alojamento peregrino varia de albergues municipais oferecendo facilidades básicas de 5 € (sem reserva prévia) para albergues privados a partir de € 10 +, mas geralmente com recursos adicionais, tais como máquinas de lavar e secar secadora. O último um benefício real em tempo de chuva. A 3 prato principal refeição básica com vinho (menu peregrino) a partir de 9 €.

Estes mapas multilingues reconhecem a irmandade internacional do Caminho. Espera-se que ajudem a forjar um sentido de camaradagem e comunhão – a partilha de uma intenção comum que está na base da peregrinação. É este objectivo transcendente que distingue uma peregrinação de uma mera caminhada.

Todos percorremos dois caminhos simultaneamente – o caminho exterior ao longo do qual transportamos o nosso corpo e um caminho interior, da alma. Devemos estar conscientes de ambos e encontrar o tempo de preparação adequada. A maneira tradicional do peregrino é viajar sozinho, a pé, carregando todas as possessões materiais necessárias para a viagem que tem pela frente. Isto proporciona a primeira lição do peregrino – deixar para trás tudo o que é supérfluo e viajar com o que é realmente necessário. A preparação para o caminho interior é semelhante – devemos começar por abandonar o lixo psíquico acumulado ao longo dos anos, os ressentimentos, os preconceitos e as crenças antiquadas. Com uma mente aberta poderemos assimilar mais facilmente as lições a tirar ao longo deste Caminho de Busca.

Há muito tempo que andamos adormecidos. Apesar do mundo caótico à nossa volta ou talvez por isso, algo está a compelir-nos para o despertar da nossa amnésia colectiva. Um sinal deste despertar é o número de pessoas atraídas pelo Caminho. O ritmo agitado da vida moderna, que sentimos tanto no nosso trabalho como na nossa vida familiar e social, atira-nos para longe de nós próprios. Deixámo-nos afastar para a periferia da nossa vida confundindo estar ocupado com estar vivo, mas esta existência superficial acaba por ser inerentemente insatisfatória.

A peregrinação oferece uma oportunidade de abrandar e dar amplitude à nossa vida. É nesse espaço mais calmo que se torna possível reflectir no significado mais profundo das nossas vidas e nas razões porque estamos aqui. O Caminho encoraja-nos a fazer a pergunta essencial – quem sou eu? E fundamentalmente dá-nos tempo para que as respostas sejam compreendidas e absorvidas. Portanto não apresse o Caminho – leve o tempo que precisar, ele pode-se tornar um ponto essencial de mudança na sua vida.

Buen camino.

Legenda do mapy używanej w tym przewodniku:

Total km — Całkowita odległość na mapie etapów

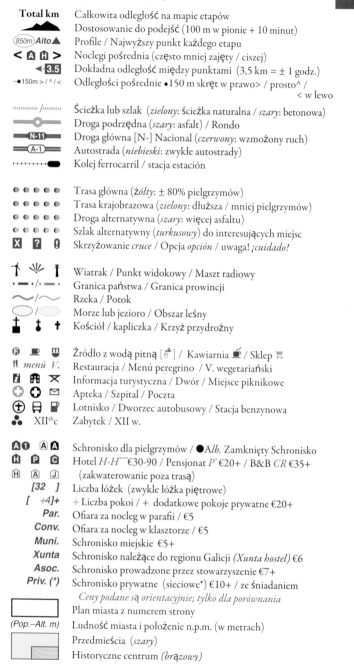 — Dostosowanie do podejść (100 m w pionie + 10 minut)

(850m) **Alto** ▲ — Profile / Najwyższy punkt każdego etapu

< ⌂ ⌂ > — Noclegi pośrednia (często mniej zajęty / ciszej)

◄ **3.5** — Dokładna odległość między punktami (3,5 km = ± 1 godz.)

→150m > / ^ / < — Odległości pośrednie •150 m skręt w prawo> / prosto^ / < w lewo

.... / .... — Ścieżka lub szlak (*zielony*: ścieżka naturalna / *szary*: betonowa)

━━○━━ — Droga podrzędna (*szary*: asfalt) / Rondo

━**N-11**━ — Droga główna [N-] Nacional (*czerwony*: wzmożony ruch)

══**A-1**══ — Autostrada (*niebieski*: zwykłe autostrady)

+++++++● — Kolej ferrocarril / stacja estación

● ● ● ● ● — Trasa główna (*żółty*: ± 80% pielgrzymów)

● ● ● ● ● — Trasa krajobrazowa (*zielony*: dłuższa / mniej pielgrzymów)

● ● ● ● ● — Droga alternatywna (*szary*: więcej asfaltu)

● ● ● ● ● — Szlak alternatywny (*turkusowy*) do interesujących miejsc

X **?** **0** — Skrzyżowanie *cruce* / Opcja *opción* / uwaga! *¡cuidado!*

↑ ☼ ↑ — Wiatrak / Punkt widokowy / Maszt radiowy

· — · / · — · — Granica państwa / Granica prowincji

~ / ~ — Rzeka / Potok

◯ / ◯ — Morze lub jezioro / Obszar leśny

♦ ♦ † — Kościół / kapliczka / Krzyż przydrożny

Ⓖ **▣** **ᵾ** — Źródło z wodą pitną [♨] / Kawiarnia ☕ / Sklep 🛒

¶ *menú V.* — Restauracja / Menú peregrino / V. wegetariański

🅩 **⊞** **✕** — Informacja turystyczna / Dwór / Miejsce piknikowe

✛ **✚** **✉** — Apteka / Szpital / Poczta

⊕ **🚌** **🅿** — Lotnisko / Dworzec autobusowy / Stacja benzynowa

••• XIIᵗʰc — Zabytek / XII w.

🅐❶ **🅐🅐** — Schronisko dla pielgrzymów / ●*Alb.* Zamknięty Schronisko

🅗 **🅟** **🅒** — Hotel *H-H***** €30-90 / Pensjonat *P** €20+ / B&B *CR* €35+

🅗 🅐 🅙 — (zakwaterowanie poza trasą)

[32] — Liczba łóżek (zwykle łóżka piętrowe)

[÷4]+ — ÷ Liczba pokoi / + dodatkowe pokoje prywatne €20+

Par. — Ofiara za nocleg w parafii / €5

Conv. — Ofiara za nocleg w klasztorze / €5

Muni. — Schronisko miejskie €5+

Xunta — Schronisko należące do regionu Galicji *(Xunta hostel)* €6

Asoc. — Schronisko prowadzone przez stowarzyszenie €7+

Priv. (*) — Schronisko prywatne (sieciowe*) €10+ / ze śniadaniem

Ceny podane są orientacyjnie; tylko dla porównania

▭ — Plan miasta z numerem strony

(Pop.–Alt. m) — Ludność miasta i położenie n.p.m. (w metrach)

▭ — Przedmieścia (*szary*)

▭ — Historyczne centrum *(brązowy)*

Wstęp: Wszyscy posiadamy zbyt dużo rzeczy: aby ulżyć w drodze, wydaliśmy ten skromny zbiór map. Było to możliwe dzięki bezinteresownej pracy stowarzyszeń pielgrzymów, które oznakowały szlaki tak, że obecnie potrzebujemy jedynie podstawowych informacji, aby dostać się do naszego celu. Byłoby to trudne, gdybyśmy stale wytężali uwagę na znalezienie wszystkich żółtych strzałek oznaczających drogę do Santiago – grunt to skupienie. Zapoznajcie się teraz z symbolami wykorzystanymi na mapach.

Wielojęzyczne mapy dowodzą istnienia międzynarodowej wspólnoty na Camino. Pomaga to rozwijać poczucie wspólnoty i braterstwa, budować wspólnotę duchową, która jest sercem pielgrzymowania. Ów niezwykły ogień odróżnia pątnika od turysty. Zalecamy zakup przewodnika ze wskazówkami, jak najlepiej przygotować się do takiej długiej wyprawy, jednego z polskich lub w poradnik *A Pilgrim's Guide to the Camino Francés*.

Wszyscy wędrujemy równocześnie dwiema ścieżkami: zewnętrzną, którą podąża nasze ciało i wewnętrzną drogą duszy. Trzeba być świadomym obydwu z nich i poświęcić czas na odpowiednie przygotowanie się. Tradycyjnym sposobem pielgrzymowania jest samotna wędrówka piesza i noszenie wszystkiego, czego potrzebujemy w drodze. To pierwsza lekcja dla pątnika: zostawić za sobą wszystko, co zbędne i podróżować jedynie z najbardziej potrzebnym wyposażeniem. Przygotowanie ścieżki wewnętrznej jest podobne: zaczynamy od pozostawienia wszelkich wewnętrznych „nieużytków" nagromadzonych przez lata, jak urazy, uprzedzenia i schematy myślowe. Otwartym umysłem i sercem łatwiej przyswoimy lekcje, które odnajdziemy na tej starej Drodze Doświadczenia.

Przez długi czas byliśmy pogrążeni w drzemce. Pomimo chaosu w otaczającym świecie albo raczej z jego powodu coś nas porusza, aby obudzić się z zapomnienia. Znakiem tego przebudzenia jest liczba ludzi, którzy są pociągani do wędrówki przez Camino. Pospieszne życie nowoczesnego świata nie tylko w naszej pracy, ale też w rodzinie i społeczeństwie, prowadzi nas na zewnątrz i pozostawia z dala od naszego wnętrza. Pozwoliliśmy się wyrzucić na powierzchnię naszego życia - myląc "bycie zajętym" z "byciem żywym". Ale ta powierzchowna egzystencja wcale nas nie cieszy.

Pielgrzymowanie daje okazję do tego, aby zwolnić i aby dać naszemu życiu trochę przestrzeni. W tej spokojniejszej przestrzeni możemy zastanowić się nad głębszym znaczeniem naszego życia i nad tym, po co istniejemy. Camino daje nam odwagę do zadawania nieprzemijających pytań: kim jestem? Oraz daje czas na odkrycie i zrozumienie odpowiedzi. A więc nie spieszcie się na Camino – dajcie sobie czas, jakiego wymaga, gdyż może stanowić punkt zwrotny w waszym życiu.

Którąkolwiek drogę wybierzemy, nasze ostateczne miejsce przeznaczenia jest pewne. Jedyny wybór, jakiego mamy dokonać, to czas, którego nam potrzeba, aby dotrzeć na *buen camino*.

12 Caminos de Santiago

❶ Camino Francés* 778 km
   St. Jean – Santiago
Camino Invierno*
Ponferrada – Santiago **275** km

❷ Chemin de Paris 1000 km
   Paris – St. Jean via Tours

❸ Chemin de Vézelay 900 km
   Vezélay – St. Jean via Bazas

❹ Chemin du Puy 740 km
   Le Puy-en-Velay – St. Jean
   Ext. to Geneva, Budapest

❺ Chemin d'Arles 750 km
   Arles – Somport Pass
Camino Aragonés **160** km
   Somport Pass – Óbanos
Camí San Jaume **600** km
   Port de Selva – Jaca
Camino del Piamonte **515** km
   Narbonne - Lourdes - St. Jean

❻ Camino de Madrid 320 km
   Madrid – Sahagún
Camino de Levante 900 km
   Valencia – Zamora
   Alt. via Cuenca – Burgos

❼ Camino Mozárabe 390 km
   Granada – Mérida
   (Málaga alt. via Baena)

❽ Via de la Plata 1,000 km
   Seville – Santiago
Camino Sanabrés Ourense **110** km

❾ Camino Portugués *Central** **640** km
   Lisboa – Porto 389 km
   Porto – Santiago 251 km
Camino Portugués *Costa** **320** km
   Porto – Santiago
   via Caminha & **Variante Espiritual***

❿ Camino Finisterre* 86 km
   Santiago – Finisterre
   via – Muxía – Santiago **114** km

⓫ Camino Inglés* 120 km
   Ferrol & Coruna – Santiago

⓬ Camino del Norte 830 km
   Irún – Santiago via Gijón
Camino Primitivo 320 km
   Oviedo – Lugo – Melide